LEAVES
from
THE WALNUT TREE

LEAVES from THE WALNUT TREE

RECIPES OF A LIFETIME

ANN & FRANCO
TARUSCHIO

PAVILION

Dedicated to Pavinee, our daughter, with our love.

•

We would like to thank Helen and Owen Forester, Ann's parents, for all the help, encouragement and tremendous support they have given us over the years, from the day we opened to the present day. To Pavinee, our daughter, thank you for bringing a new dimension and great joy to our lives. To our friend Jill Norman, thank you for your skilful and patient job as editor, and for your words of encouragement during the writing of this book. To Sarah van Niekerk for supplying the beautiful wood engravings. To Gillian Young, senior commissioning editor at Pavilion, thank you for believing we had a book worth publishing. Thank you also to Jan Morris for writing the foreword, and to all our customers and friends who have been so loyal to us during our past thirty years.

First published in Great Britain in 1993 by
Pavilion Books Limited
26 Upper Ground, London SE1 9PD

Designed by Peter Luff

A CIP catalogue record for this book is
available from the British Library

ISBN 1 85145 097 5

Printed and bound in Great Britain by Butler & Tanner Ltd

2 4 6 8 10 9 7 5 3 1

This book may be ordered by post direct from
the publisher. Please contact the Marketing
Department. But try your bookshop first.

CONTENTS

FOREWORD

It is a dangerous thing when a restaurant becomes an Institution. It implies a certain hardening of arteries and petrification of style, not to mention a perilous access of pomposity. No such hazard, however, attends The Walnut Tree at Llandewi Skirrid, which is an institution indeed, but is insuperably young of spirit, flexible of response and unpretentious. Among all the great restaurants I spend too much of my money frequenting, The Walnut Tree is the most fun.

This is partly because of its location. It is an old pub on a country road a few miles out of Abergavenny (Y Fenni to Welsh-speakers), in the lovely border country where Wales meets England. The wild Black Mountains stand behind it, comfortable pasture-lands stand in front, and not far to the south is the famously high-spirited country known generically as the Valleys, where the coal used to be mined, and where the Welsh are at their most ebullient. Such a combination of landscapes and environments certainly helps, when it comes to giving a restaurant character.

Then there is the exuberance of its proprietors. Franco Taruschio is Italian, Ann Taruschio is English, and both are tempered (or so I like to think, as a proud Welsh patriot) by the happier influences of Welshness. Between them they give the place an atmosphere of mingled authority, festivity and relaxation. Nothing could be more professionally run than The Walnut Tree, but so easy do the Taruschios make it appear, so delightfully family-like is their staff of local ladies, that a visit to this restaurant always seems to me like a celebratory evening out with old friends.

Many of the customers *are* old friends – there are regulars at The Walnut Tree who dined here on the very evening the restaurant opened, in the bitter winter of 1963. Now that the place is famous clients come from everywhere, but for my tastes the charm of The Walnut Tree lies still in its affectionate cadre of local people: farmers, doctors, business people from the neighbouring towns, other Italian restaurateurs, media bravos from Cardiff, merrily flamboyant parties from the Valleys.

All this makes for a certain magic, but the real miracle is this: that for all its laid-back feel this is an extremely sophisticated restaurant. It knows exactly what it is up to. It knows that Armani suits do not a gourmet (or a gentleman) make. Its standards are subtle and civilized, and in its humorous understanding of social values, its patrician disregard of trend or showiness, it is matched in my experience only by Harry's Bar in Venice.

Although I myself would happily go to The Walnut Tree for a plate of scrambled eggs, I realize that for most people it is the food that counts. Somehow or other, though, here more than in most restaurants food and ambience coincide. The Walnut Tree cuisine is as amiable as the atmosphere, and has long been celebrated. Stars and laurel wreaths and little black bottles mark its progress through the restaurant guides, and Elizabeth David gave it the accolade of declaring The Walnut Tree her favourite restaurant in Great Britain.

I tried to analyse the cuisine once, by identifying the origins of a particular night's menu, and found a Belgian soup, a Thai way of doing Dover sole, a fish soup from Ancona, a Sicilian cheesecake, Scandinavian gravlax, English partridge, Malakoff torte, Welsh salted duck and Italian-Jewish home-cured beef. But all is given a distinctive unity by Franco Taruschio's cooking, which food critics universally agree to be unique. With herbs from the garden behind the pub, fruits and vegetables from local growers, fish and meat from a supplier down the road, the victuals at The Walnut Tree are, like the restaurant itself, a fascinating blend of the worldly and the simple, the plain organic and the exquisitely invented.

And yet this is an Institution! *Leaves from The Walnut Tree* will give you an inkling of how it has become so widely admired a restaurant, but you must read between its lines and recipes to discover by what alchemy The Walnut Tree has managed to retain, through all its fame, a character so kind, so entertaining and so full of integrity.

Jan Morris, 1993

Introduction

Until 1963, the year we bought The Walnut Tree Inn, Franco had been working in a hotel in Rugby. He had trained at a then famous hotel school in Bellagio, Como, Italy, one of the first hotel schools to open after the war. Through the hotel school he had done a *stage* in Switzerland, then France and had come to England to learn English to further his career in Italy. I had been teaching first in Rugby then in Wolverhampton. We met and all Franco's plans changed, he opted to stay here and get married. We then decided that if we were ever going to see each other when we got married we had better buy a business straight away.

That summer was spent searching for a property within our means. Eventually in October we found The Walnut Tree Inn. It was a pleasant little pub 3 miles from Abergavenny on a B road. We had dreamed of having a restaurant only but realized that it was difficult to obtain a licence for unlicensed premises and existing restaurants for sale were few and far between, so better to buy a pub and add a restaurant on. The pub seemed a good idea. It would already have a trade, so while we were building up the restaurant we would be making money from the licensed trade side of it. This turned out to be a very important aspect, as after the purchase of the inn we only had a little money left to our names. One thing we did have was tremendous confidence and enthusiasm that we could make a restaurant work in the wilds of nowhere. On 9 November 1963 we got married and on 13 November 1963 we moved into The Walnut Tree Inn.

The first few months were hilarious, with Franco the Italian trying to be mine host. He could not understand what the local customers were saying to him and they could not understand him! They also thought the food he cooked was decidedly odd. Whenever they smelt garlic coming from the kitchen they would mutter into their pints of beer. In the beginning we were so busy decorating, we had little time for cooking but we did manage to roast chickens with rosemary and garlic which we served with rolls. As we got ourselves more organized, we introduced lasagne, cannelloni and spaghetti bolognese.

It was nearing Christmas 1963 and we still had not got the restaurant going. A week before Christmas family friends rang to ask if we would do Christmas lunch for them. We explained that our dining room was not ready yet but they would not take no for an answer. We explained that we had no dining table, and worse still we had not enough money to buy one. No problem, the friends made us a gift of a beautiful large Georgian table. We did have some chairs which was something! Next problem, not enough cutlery. My mother lent us hers, and so it went on. Christmas Eve we finished decorating, laid the carpet, hung the curtains and put the furniture in. The Walnut Tree dining room was ready for business.

Over the next few months we added 2 more tables and were now able to seat 14 in the dining room. Our fourth table came about because of a confusion over a name, Davies. Two Dr Davies's from Abergavenny had booked for a party of four, but we thought only one Dr Davies had booked, until they rang in with their orders. To save our faces Franco had quickly to bang a few nails into a bit of wood to extend a small table we had found in an outhouse. When the second Dr Davies came in I had to whisper to him, "Don't lean too heavily on the table, it might collapse!" The following day we bought a proper table! Now we could seat 18.

Our Christmas Day experience had given us more confidence and we were now more determined than ever to concentrate on the food side. Our solicitor, doctor, dentist, local pharmacist, vet and a couple of dozen other local customers did a great deal to boost our revenue. They told friends about us who in turn told friends and so it snowballed on. Talking of snow, during the New Year of 1964 it snowed and we thought no one would get to us. On the first night of the snow, we had a party of 12 booked. Round about 5 o'clock it started to snow; it snowed and snowed. The telephone lines came down, the road became impassable, Franco and I looked at each other in despair: the food would be wasted as surely no one could get to us. 8 o'clock came and twelve "snowmen" with shovels walked in. They had walked the 3 miles from Abergavenny determined not to let us down. What a night.

In 1964 Egon Ronay awarded us two stars in this *Guide to Good Eating*. We were still doing everything ourselves with family coming over at the weekends to help—mother at the stove, father, sister, a cousin and friends assisting whoever needed them the most. We hit on the idea of sending menus when people booked and asking them to order on the morning they were coming; this meant no waste. Each day we would go to Abergavenny with a huge donkey basket to purchase the food. We had to go by bus as we still had no car. We started to employ staff; one of them is still with us. By the end of 1964 we knew we were on the right track.

People had said we were crazy when we decided to buy The Walnut Tree. How could a restaurant of the type we intended to create survive in such a rural situation? We had done our homework. We knew the Heads of the Valleys road was being built, opening up the Welsh valleys and making easy access to Abergavenny. The Severn bridge would be opening a few years later, making access to Wales very easy. We are 25 minutes from the bridge. The opening of the bridge brought in a flood of customers and brought big changes to the area around us. Welsh farmhouses and cottages were snapped up as second homes, many by expatriate Welsh needing to have a foot in Wales even if only just over the border.

When we first started cooking, dishes like lasagne and cannelloni were treated with suspicion. Few people knew what to expect. Thirty years ago these dishes were virtually unknown to the British population; only a few who had travelled to Italy had tried them. These dishes always had to be described in great detail before people would try them, but try them they did and came again for more. Elizabeth David's book *Italian Food* had made a great impact on people in England but on only a few in Wales. Customers came in the beginning out of curiosity. They had heard about this couple who cooked "odd" food in the middle of the Welsh countryside, or as the English journalists put it, on the side of a brackeny hill! We had one brave customer who ate minestrone followed by lasagne followed by cannelloni, because he believed the Italians only ate pasta! He is still eating at The Walnut Tree and we often laugh together about that meal. He is now a very knowledgeable customer.

Word went round and customers started to flock to us. If there was no chair space they sat on the floor and ate, or leaned on the bonnets of their cars and ate. It was crazy but exciting. The customers who came in the early days and enjoyed our food are still coming to us now. We have seen their children grow up and grandchildren arrive. The menu when we first started was half Italian, half French. The French influence came from our experiences in France; Franco had worked for a year in a restaurant in Clermont-Ferrand and I had been to a finishing school just outside Lille. As the years passed, the French influence decreased and then another influence crept in.

In 1976 we approached the Thai authorities regarding the adoption of a Thai baby. It seemed for a while we stood more chance of adopting an older child so we started to learn the Thai language and study Thai foods. Eventually we heard we were to have a baby, not an older child. The language got forgotten but not the food and a few slightly westernized Thai dishes appeared on our menu. A few years later, British chefs started to incorporate Thai spices into their food.

Pavinee, our adopted daughter, loves Thai food despite being weaned in Bangkok by Irish nuns on Irish stew! Over the years at The Walnut Tree we have befriended many foreign students and lonely wives of foreigners working in the UK—Vietnamese, mainland Chinese, Japanese, Greek, Thai, Spanish, Sri Lankan and Ukrainian. They have all had an influence on our menu, however small. To cook together is a wonderful way of communication, no language barriers there. Many a happy hour has been spent learning the culinary techniques of another country. Of course the strongest influence has always been Franco's cooking from the Marche region of Italy. This is the food of hard-working people who love their beautiful countryside, an area not unlike the part we live in in Wales. Pasta, fish and game are strong in his region's cooking and have always dominated our menus, according to the seasons. The cooking of the Marche is simple and unadulterated, varied and healthy, always using the freshest of ingredients from the sea, mountains and fields, and strongly flavoured with herbs.

The Marche is where the North and the South meet, so the cooking is influenced by both. Here in the Marches of Wales, we also have the influences of sea, mountains and fields, so it has been comparatively easy to adapt Marchigiani cooking using local ingredients. In 1970 we doubled the size of the dining room and the bistro bar and, due to pressure from the customers, gave up our bar menu and offered the dining room menu to people eating in the bistro bar. Customers who eat in the bistro are free to eat one course if they should so wish. We are still serving lasagne as we did thirty years ago but we no longer have to explain what it is! Customers no longer have to be cajoled into trying a new dish. We now have customers coming to us from all over the world. The media discovered us and gave us a tremendous boost. We have never thought of leaving The Walnut Tree, it has offered us everything: the great pleasure of working in a beautiful area, loyal staff and loyal customers. Our great desire has always been to offer good food in a simple non-stuffy, relaxing atmosphere. We hope that is what our customers think we have achieved. The recipes in this book are some of the recipes we have cooked over thirty years.

Ann Taruschio,

The Walnut Tree Inn, 1993

HINTS ON COOKING

Cooking times can never be definitive; they can vary for many reasons. They vary according to the type of cooking vessels used, the type of metal they are made from, the thickness of the vessels, and also the type of heat used. Always keep an eye on what is cooking. If the sauce is reducing too much, lower the heat and add more liquid. Always taste as you are cooking. A little more salt may be needed or a boost from a herb or pepper.

Here are some notes on the ingredients most basic to our recipes. Notes to other important ingredients appear throughout the recipes where relevant.

BALSAMIC VINEGAR Aceto balsamico *is made from the cooked concentrated must of the white Trebbiano grape, which has been harvested as late as possible so as to take advantage of every last bit of summer sun. It is then aged in casks of different woods, first in oak then in chestnut, cherry, ash and finally mulberry. By law,* aceto balsamico *must be aged at least 10 years before it can be sold. Some very old vintages of* aceto balsamico *are available and in Italy they are prized like good vintages of wine.*

It is a dark brown vinegar with a fluid syrup-like consistency and a very aromatic fragrance, sharp but sweet. Try it sprinkled on very ripe, halved strawberries, with a little sugar, as they do in Modena where this vinegar originates.

A simple fettina *(thin slice) of steak quickly*

fried in olive oil, seasoned and a dash or two of balsamic vinegar sprinkled on afterwards is good as well. It can also be used mixed with olive oil as a dressing for salads.

TOMATOES *We usually use plum tomatoes in our recipes. They are easily available during the summer months in this country. In the winter months, plum tomatoes are not so easily available and ordinary tomatoes seem to dominate the greengrocers shelves, under-ripe and tasteless. Buy the tomatoes before you need them and allow them to ripen off. Always try to use tomatoes which are as red and ripe as possible.*

Here is a little tip when making tomato coulis/ sauce, during the months when the tomatoes are not so good. In a frying pan heat up some extra-virgin olive oil, enough to make a thin film across the base of the frying pan, until it is very hot—a haze should rise from it. Add some chopped tomatoes and let them sizzle for a few minutes, then fry them until they are soft. Add a tablespoon or so of tomato purée, depending on the redness of the tomatoes, to every 450g/1lb of tomatoes. Season with salt and pepper. Pass through a food mill.

The act of sizzling the tomatoes brings out the natural sugar in them and slightly caramelizes it, thus sweetening the rather dull tomatoes. The extra-virgin olive oil will impart a wonderful flavour to the sauce.

There is a little story from Romagna which goes as follows. There was once a priest who was always poking his nose into other people's affairs, not with malice—just simple nosiness. The parishioners who were nevertheless very fond of him nicknamed him Don Pomodoro (Dom Tomato) because, like the tomato, he was into everything.

PARMESAN *Parmesan, which is made from cow's milk, has been made the same way for hundreds of years in the Emilia Romagna region of Italy. It is an absolute essential in Italian cooking, imparting a special flavour to the dishes. It will be noticed that we always say freshly grated Parmesan cheese. Buy a large piece of Parmesan. It will not deteriorate rapidly if kept properly. Cut it up into smallish pieces, then wrap them in 2–3 thicknesses of tinfoil. It will keep well on a low shelf in the refrigerator. Never buy already grated cheese. Parmesan cheese which has been previously grated loses some of its flavour and goes rancid quite quickly.*

An electric cheese grater can be bought in Italy, making the job of grating very easy. Less cheese is wasted using an electric grater as it will grate very close to the hard skin. Look out for one on a trip to Italy. Perhaps someone will start to import them to the UK now we are using more Parmesan.

OLIVE OIL *In most of our recipes we use extra-virgin olive oil, which is dense and strong in flavour. At home in the Marche we go straight to the* frantoio, *the olive oil press, to buy the simply pressed oil. Sometimes the reader will notice we have only written olive oil. By this we mean a light olive oil, because an oil that is much lighter in body and flavour is needed for the dish.*

Olive oil has been used in Mediterranean countries for thousands of years but only in recent years has it become so popular outside these countries, ever since the discovery that it protects us against diseases of the heart and arteries. It is also rich in vitamin E which slows down the aging process of the skin and bones.

Olive oil is the only oil made from a fruit, and olive trees with their gnarled and twisted trunks, magnificent with their silvery green foliage, are symbolic of strength, faith, and peace. There is a story in the Old Testament that a dove sent out from the Ark returned with an olive branch in its beak, a sign that peace had been made between man and nature. Together with bread and wine, olive oil and olives are an integral part of Italian life. There is an Italian saying: 'What love, olive oil and wine can't cure, God help you.'

TRUFFLES *We are able to bring* tartufi *(truffles) of one species or another all year round from the Marche. From 1 October to the middle of December there is the famed* tartufo bianco pregiato. *The white truffle is the truffle most prized by the Italians. It has a very strong distinct aroma, difficult to describe.*

White truffles are always used raw as a condiment and are best on bland dishes; they dissolve in the mouth. We have had a few funny experiences with white truffles. Once on a fleeting visit to Italy, Franco could not resist purchasing a few kilos of white truffles. He asked the tartufaio to wrap them in newspaper and then seal them well in a polystyrene box. Despite being winter, it was a hot afternoon. When we arrived at Bologna Airport our luggage with the truffles buried inside was checked through; we showed our documents for the truffles to the customs officer on duty and through we went to the departure lounge. The intended time of our departure came and went. I heard two carabinieri mention my husband's name ... he was fast asleep. Suddenly over the tannoy: "Signor Franco Taruschio per favore." Quickly I awakened Franco. Two big burly carabinieri came towards him, machine guns slung over their shoulders, and marched him off. He was taken to a hangar where his suitcase was placed in the middle. No one spoke. Three more carabinieri joined them with Alsatian dogs straining on their leads. One of the carabinieri turned to Franco and said, "We believe you have some kind of gas in your suitcase." Franco laughed. "No, no, it's truffles."

"Open your suitcase then."

As Franco bent down to open his case, he heard the guns being cocked ... He prayed: please don't let their fingers slip! Frantically he opened the box, the truffles tumbled out. There was relieved laughter all round. The dogs sent into the hold of the plane to check for bombs or drugs had smelt the truffles and gone crazy. No wonder they use dogs in Italy to scent out the prized truffle.

The Marche is also famed for the tartufo nero pregiato, the Perigord-type truffle and the less precious variety of tartufo nero scorzone, the summer truffle. The black truffle is entirely *different to the white truffle: it has a herbaceous and spicy flavour and a chewy texture. The black truffle is cooked to bring out its perfume which complements many dishes.*

We have always bought our truffles from St Angelo in Vado, a small town situated in the Pesarese Appenines, a mountainous chain with three valleys, each with a river flowing down to the Adriatic sea. A local legend has it that in 1668 Cardinal Cesare Rasponi, when resident in Urbino, an ancient university town near St Angelo, sent a gift of two truffles to his cousin Cardinal Flavio Chigi, nephew of Pope Alessandro VII. These truffles weighed 18 kilos and 34 kilos respectively. They were supposed to have been found on the estate of Filippo Cortese da Bologna. So for centuries this area has been known for its abundance of truffles.

ANTIPASTI

Antipasto, which means before the main course, not before the pasta as is commonly thought in this country, is not usually served at home in Italy. It is reserved for restaurant consumption. At home a few slices of salami or a slice or two of Parma ham with figs or melon would be served. On the Marchigiani coast the antipasti are usually based on fish; inland, vegetables and meat are used. Our antipasti are a mixture of Italian, Welsh and Thai recipes, fish still being the predominant ingredient.

Zuppa is not part of the antipasti table. In Italy it is served instead of pasta. We have included zuppa in our antipasti section, as at The Walnut Tree it is generally eaten as a first course. Soups in Italy come under two headings: zuppa *or* minestra. *Zuppa in Italy would mean a thick soup, not creamed, ladled over bread. Minestra usually has pasta or rice added to it. We have used the word zuppa for all our soups; although not correct it is easier to follow.*

SOLE GOUJONS WITH THAI DIP

SERVES 4

575g/1¼lb fillets Dover sole (cod can be substituted for the sole)

225g/8oz Japanese breadcrumbs (obtainable in Oriental supermarkets)

4 eggs beaten with 8 tablespoons of cold water

salt and freshly ground black pepper

flour

oil for deep-frying

Cut the fillets of Dover sole into thinnish strips (little finger thick). Dip the strips in flour and shake off any excess.

•

Season the eggs with salt and pepper. Add the water and beat lightly with a fork. Dip goujons into the egg and then into the Japanese breadcrumbs. Deep fry the goujons in hot oil, until golden. Drain on absorbent paper. Serve with Thai dip (prik nam pla).

•

JAPANESE BREADCRUMBS *Flaked breadcrumbs which are freeze-dried as opposed to baked. This process prevents the oil from soaking into the crumb.*

KRATONG COCKTAIL CUPS

MAKES AROUND 30 CUPS

90g/3oz rice flour

90g/3oz plain flour

2 cups cold water

oil for frying

Kratong are little batter cups which originate in Thailand. A pie tee mould looks like a mini fluted fairy cake tin on a long handle. To speed up the process of making these cups, 4-cup pie tee moulds can be bought from most Thai grocers.

•

Add the water gradually to the sifted flours, stirring until smooth. Heat vegetable oil for deep-frying and dip a pie tee mould into the hot oil for a couple of seconds or so. Remove the mould from the oil and immediately dip it into the batter. Do not allow batter to get inside the mould. Then dip the mould back into the oil and fry until the batter cups are crisp. Gently remove the cups from the moulds. This operation takes a bit of time to master, but is easy once you get the hang of it.

•

To serve, fill each cup with a teaspoonful of the Thai pork mixture (page 26). Decorate in the same way, that is with a little chilli and a coriander leaf.

CHILLI WITH FISH SAUCE
PRIK NAM PLA

6 tablespoons nam pla (fish sauce)

4 red Serrano chillies, seeded and finely chopped

2 teaspoons granulated sugar

6 tablespoons fresh lime juice

2 cloves garlic, crushed

Mix all the ingredients together.

•

NAM PLA *A thin translucent brown sauce made either from fish, octopus or prawns. The fish are salted and fermented in jars and the liquid which results from the fermentation is extracted and bottled. Nam pla is rich in B vitamins and protein. No salt is needed when this sauce is used. Nam pla is to the Thais what soy sauce is to the Chinese.*

THAI PORK APPETIZER

SERVES 6

450g/1lb minced pork

2 tablespoons peanut oil

4 cloves garlic, finely chopped

2 shallots, finely chopped

3 coriander roots, finely chopped

1 teaspoon freshly ground black pepper

60g/2oz granulated sugar

115g/4oz roasted peanuts, coarsely chopped

1 teaspoon nam pla (fish sauce)

18 lettuce cups from a crisp lettuce

2 red chillies, seeded and sliced thinly

coriander leaves

36 orange segments

In a wok, heat the peanut oil and fry the garlic, shallots, coriander root and pepper until it gives off a pungent aroma. Add the pork and stir-fry for 4–5 minutes. Add the sugar and stir in. The pork will take on a shiny appearance at this point. Stir in the peanuts and mix in thoroughly. Season with 1 tablespoon of nam pla.

•

To serve, put 3 lettuce cups on each plate and fill each cup with 4 tablespoons of the pork mixture. Garnish the meat with chilli and coriander leaves. Place 6 orange segments between the lettuce cups.

Crostini of Cotechino with Chutney
CROSTINI DI COTECHINO CON CHUTNEY

Boil the cotechino (page 170). Toast the crostini, slice the cotechino while still hot and place a slice on each crostini. Serve with a spoonful of tomato and onion chutney (see below) on top.

•

CROSTINI *Small rounds of bread either toasted or cooked on the griddle. Use French stick bread for these. Crostoni are double the size of crostini.*

SERVES 3

1 cotechino (page 170) weighing 300g/10oz

12 crostini cut from a French stick, 4 per person

Tomato and Onion Chutney
POMODORO E CIPOLLA CHUTNEY

Peel and de-seed the tomatoes and cut each into 8 sections. Peel the onions and cut each into 8 sections, then blanch. Caramelize the sugar with 1 tablespoon of the vinegar. Add the blanched onion and tomato. Toss the tomato and onion in the caramel, reduce the caramel by half, then add the remaining vinegar and reduce to a syrup.

•

This chutney is not for storing. It is best used fresh and keeps for 3–4 days only.

100g/3½oz semi ripe tomatoes

100g/3½oz small red onions

60g/2oz sugar

2½ tablespoons red wine vinegar

Crostini with Finely Chopped Mushrooms, Garlic and Herbs

CROSTINI DI FUNGHI TRIFOLATI

MAKES 50 CROSTINI
25 BRUSCHETTA

1.4kg/3lb field mushrooms, or cultivated ones

115g/4oz butter

2 large onions, finely chopped

4 cloves garlic, finely chopped

¼pt dry white wine

salt and freshly ground black pepper

2 heaped tablespoons chopped parsley

½ teaspoon chopped thyme

nutmeg

Melt the butter and fry the onion and garlic until golden. Add the mushrooms, roughly chopped, and fry. Pour in the wine and season with salt and pepper. Drain off the liquor from the mushrooms and reduce to a thick syrupy texture. Pass the mushrooms through a food processor until chopped finely, like grains, then return the mushrooms to the liquor, add parsley, thyme and nutmeg. Check the seasoning. This mixture should be firm, not sloppy.

•

Serve on top of crostini (small rounds of bread, lightly buttered and toasted in the oven until pale gold). It is also good served on bruschetta (this is a thick slice of bread cut from a round loaf of country bread, grilled on charcoal or on a griddle, rubbed with garlic and then olive oil dribbled over it).

Crostini with Peppers and Sausage
CROSTINI CON PEPERONI E SALSICCE

SERVES 12 AS ANTIPASTO
6 AS A MAIN COURSE

6 red peppers

360g/12oz Marchigiani sausage meat (page 169)

2 cups fresh breadcrumbs

2 cups milk

2 eggs

2 tablespoons fresh breadcrumbs

6–12 crostini

garlic

extra-virgin olive oil

Wash the peppers, cut in half, remove the seeds and veins. Put them on an oiled baking tray and put in an oven preheated at 200°C/400°F/gas 6 for 10 minutes. Leave to cool. Soak the 2 cups of breadcrumbs in the milk and squeeze out the milk. Mix the bread with the sausage meat, add the eggs and mix well.

•

Stuff the peppers with the mixture, sprinkle over the 2 tablespoons of fresh breadcrumbs and drizzle extra-virgin olive oil on top.

•

Bake in an oven set at 200°C/400°F/gas 6 for 15 minutes. Serve on toasted crostini rubbed with a little garlic and a drizzle of extra-virgin olive oil on top.

BRUSCHETTA WITH SEAFOOD
BRUSCHETTA CON FRUTTI DI MARE

SERVES 4

500g/1lb 2oz fresh mussels

60g/2oz cooked squid cut in rings

16 cooked peeled prawns

6 fillets anchovies, roughly chopped

2 cloves garlic, finely chopped

1 tablespoon parsley, finely chopped

2 tablespoons extra-virgin olive oil

20g/¾oz sun-dried tomatoes in olive oil, cut in julienne

30 black olives, pitted

1 generous pinch dried chilli flakes

salt and freshly ground black pepper to taste

8 fresh basil leaves

Wash and remove the beards from the mussels. Place the mussels in a shallow pan, cover the pan and leave over high heat until the mussels have opened. Remove the mussels from the shells, reserving 4 in their shell for decoration. Strain and reserve the mussel liquor.

•

Fry the garlic and parsley briefly in the olive oil, add the sun-dried tomatoes and the olives, fry for a few seconds. Add 2 tablespoons of the mussel liquor.

•

Add all the fish, warm them through, season with salt, pepper and chilli flakes. Serve on slices of bruschetta. Decorate with shreds of fresh basil and a mussel in a shell.

•

BRUSCHETTA *Thick slices of bread cut from a large round loaf of bread, cooked on a griddle, rubbed with garlic and dressed with extra-virgin olive oil. This is the basic recipe but other dressings can be used.*

Egg and Chicken Broth
STRACCIATELLE

Beat the eggs in a bowl, add the remaining dry ingredients. Dilute the egg mixture with a cup of cold stock, blend in well.

•

Bring the remaining stock to the boil, pour in the egg mixture, and stir thoroughly with a fork. Lower the heat, simmer for 2 minutes, breaking the egg up with a fork, so that it looks like little rags. (Stracciatelle means little rags.) Serve boiling hot with more Parmesan cheese.

Thirty years ago in early February, I (Franco) took my wife home to meet my parents in Italy. My mother prepared a meal which was repeated many times over the years for weary travellers. The table would be covered with a linen cloth and napkins, which she had woven from linen she had spun 35 years previously, as part of her bottom drawer. To start she would bring a steaming bowl of stracciatelle soup, the broth made from a free-range chicken. To follow, the boiled chicken would be served with extra-virgin olive oil, freshly ground black pepper and home-cured black olives, ulive strinate, *a speciality of the Marche region. The freshly picked black olives are put in a sack with sea salt and hung outside for 40 days in the frosty weather. To serve they are washed, dried and quickly fried in extra-virgin olive oil with crushed garlic, chilli flakes and zest of orange.*

SERVES 6

3 eggs

pinch of salt and freshly ground black pepper

4 tablespoons fine fresh white breadcrumbs

pinch of freshly grated nutmeg

finely grated rind of 1 lemon

4 tablespoons freshly grated Parmesan cheese

1½ litres/2½pt chicken stock

There would also be a side salad of bitter herbs and endive, plenty of unsalted bread and jugs of white wine from my father's vineyard. As we were eating our chicken, my mother would be baking apples on the baking stone at the side of the open fire. The apples would be stuffed with dried figs, honey, a little cinnamon and zest of orange with a little knob of butter, and when the apples were ready a little Strega liqueur was poured over.

Replete, we would sit by the dying embers of the fire, tired after our journey but comforted by the food and the warming glass of grappa with which we finished. My mother would bring down a clay pot with wire knitted round it, fill it with the embers of the fire—apple and grapevine wood. The pot would be slipped into a metal and wooden frame which was placed inside our bed. Half an hour later, the bed now warm, we would stagger up the stairs, remove the bed warmer and snuggle into the homespun linen sheets smelling of lavender and apple wood. A heavy rug from the Abruzzi thrown over the bed, warm and full of well-being, we would drift to sleep.

Artichoke Soup
ZUPPA DI CARCIOFI

Chop the artichokes in half and boil them in salted water until cooked, then drain. Remove the hard leaves and purée the artichokes in a food processor. The artichokes must be very young for this soup. The choke will not have developed. Add the purée to the vegetable stock and gently boil for 15 minutes. Pass the soup through a mouli-légume, discard any fibrous matter. Season the soup with salt and freshly ground black pepper, stir in the single cream and bring the soup back to just under boiling point. Serve the soup with thinly sliced toasted French bread, half an artichoke trifolati, and slivers of Parmesan.

SERVES 4

8 small young artichokes, preferably purple

½ litre/16fl oz vegetable stock

salt and freshly ground black pepper

250ml/8fl oz single cream

toast, thinly sliced

2 artichoke trifolati (see overleaf)

Parmesan cheese

VEGETABLE STOCK

Sweat 450g/1lb of onions, 450g/1lb carrots, 450g/1lb leeks, 4 stalks of celery, all roughly chopped, in a little olive oil. Pour onto the vegetables 1½litres/2pt of hot water, add a bouquet garni, season with salt and a few peppercorns. Bring the stock to the boil, reduce the heat and simmer the stock for 2 hours. Strain the stock and reserve.

ARTICHOKE TRIFOLATI

Remove all tough leaves from 2 small purple artichokes, trim the tops. Trim and scrape the stalks, leaving 2.5cm/1in. Boil the artichokes in salted water with a drop of olive oil until tender. Keep testing the artichokes. Drain them well, cut them in half and dress with extra-virgin olive oil, a little chopped parsley, 1 crushed clove of garlic, salt and freshly ground black pepper to taste. Leave the artichokes to marinate in this mixture for at least 1 hour. These artichokes can be made the day before if needed.

SWEETCORN SOUP

SERVES 4

750g/1½lb sweetcorn kernels

450ml/¾pt chicken stock

3 shallots, finely chopped

600ml/1pt milk

salt and freshly ground white pepper to taste

This is a wonderful summer soup. Very delicate and loved by young children.

•

Bring the chicken stock to the boil and add the uncooked sweetcorn kernels and shallots. Cook until the kernels are tender—about 5 minutes if young—be careful not to overcook the sweetcorn. Pour sweetcorn kernels and stock into a blender, blend until smooth.

•

Heat the milk, then add the sweetcorn mixture to the milk and season with salt and pepper. If the soup is a bit too thick, add a little more stock. Should the soup not be absolutely smooth, pass it through a sieve.

PASTA AND BEAN SOUP
PASTA E FAGIOLI

Put 2 litres/3½pt of water in a heavy saucepan which has a well fitting lid, add the borlotti beans, ham hock, onion, garlic, celery, rosemary (wrapped in muslin), parsley and olive oil. Bring to the boil, lower the heat and gently cook the beans for 1½ hours. Discard the ham hock, and rosemary, remove the vegetables and blend them. Put half of the beans through a food mill or liquidizer and return the purée to the soup of beans and vegetables. Do not replace the lid. Season with freshly ground black pepper and check the seasoning: salt may not be necessary. Bring back to the boil. Add the pasta and cook until al dente. Serve with a dash of extra-virgin olive oil and a pinch of chilli pepper to taste.

SERVES 4

300g/10oz fresh borlotti beans or 200g/7oz dried borlotti beans, presoaked

1 ham hock

200g/7oz small tubular pasta

1 onion

2 cloves garlic

2 stalks celery

1 sprig rosemary

2 sprigs parsley

125ml/4 fl oz extra-virgin olive oil

freshly ground black pepper, and salt if necessary

dried chilli flakes

Potato and Cep Soup
ZUPPA DI PATATE E PORCINI

SERVES 4

200g/7oz porcini, finely diced

5 medium potatoes

2 cloves garlic

60g/2oz butter

1 cup single cream

1–2 tablespoons finely chopped parsley

freshly grated Parmesan cheese

1 white truffle, shaved (optional)

salt and freshly ground black pepper

Peel and roughly chop the potatoes, boil them in salted water with the garlic. Leave the potatoes to cook until they start to disintegrate. Pass the potatoes, cooking water and garlic through a food mill, return to the heat. Add half the butter, salt and freshly ground black pepper. Beat the mixture with a balloon whisk; if the mixture is too thick add some more water.

•

A few minutes before serving, add the porcini mushrooms which have been sautéed in the remaining butter, the cream and parsley. Check the seasoning. Serve with Parmesan cheese and shavings of white truffle if available.

Barley Soup
ZUPPA D'ORZO

Soak the pearl barley for 2 hours in plenty of cold water.

•

In a heavy pan with a lid, fry the carrot, onion and celery in the oil and butter until softened. Add the diced prosciutto and stir in with a wooden spoon. Drain the barley and rinse it, then add the barley to the vegetable and prosciutto mixture, stir for 5 minutes. Add the stock and bay leaf and bring to the boil. Reduce the heat, put the lid on the pan and cook the soup gently for 1½ hours, stirring regularly. Towards the end of the cooking time, check the seasoning and add salt and freshly ground black pepper. Just before serving, stir in the Parmesan cheese and parsley.

SERVES 6

200g/7oz pearl barley

100g/3½oz slice prosciutto, chopped in fine dice

15g/½oz butter

25ml/1fl oz extra-virgin olive oil

1 carrot, finely chopped

1 onion, finely chopped

1 stick celery, finely chopped

1 bay leaf

2.7 litres/4½pt meat stock

salt and freshly ground black pepper

30g/1oz freshly ground Parmesan cheese

1 tablespoon finely chopped parsley

CLAM SOUP
ZUPPA DI VONGOLE

SERVES 4

2½ litres/4pt small clams (vongole) or cockles

6 shallots, finely chopped

2 cloves garlic, finely chopped

2 tablespoons extra-virgin olive oil

3 sprigs parsley, finely chopped

1 small sprig thyme

pinch of freshly ground black pepper

150ml/¼pt dry white wine

wedges of lemon

It is advisable to leave clams and cockles in plenty of water with a good handful of fine oatmeal stirred into it. This helps to clean the shellfish of sand. Leave for at least 4 hours. Then leave under running cold water for 10 minutes or so. Drain the clams and reject any that are open.

•

Sauté the shallots and garlic in 2 tablespoons of olive oil for 2–3 minutes, add the parsley, thyme, pepper and wine and allow to reduce a little over a brisk heat.

•

Add the clams and when they have opened remove the saucepan immediately. Serve this soup with wedges of lemon.

Cream of Leek and Truffle Soup
CREMA DI PORRO AL TARTUFO

Use vegetable, not chicken, stock for a vegetarian dish.

•

Cut the leeks into rings and wash thoroughly. Dice the potatoes. Sweat the leeks in 3 tablespoons of olive oil, add the potato and stir into the leeks for a few minutes. Add the stock and milk. Season and gently simmer for 45 minutes, or until potatoes are cooked. Transfer the soup to a liquidizer, add the cream and liquidize for 1 minute. Return the soup to the heat, bring to just under boiling point. Divide the soup between 6 deep soup bowls, put toasted bread on top and cover with cheese. Pass lightly under a hot grill. Shave white truffle on top.

SERVES 6

250g/9oz leeks, white and pale green parts only

500g/1lb 2oz floury potatoes

1 litre/1¾pt strong vegetable or chicken stock

325ml/12fl oz milk

150ml/¼pt single cream

100g/3½oz Fontina cheese, grated

6 slices French stick, toasted

olive oil

salt and freshly ground white pepper

1 white truffle

BELGIAN LEEK SOUP

SERVES 4

115g/4oz bacon, finely chopped

4 large leeks, white parts only, finely chopped

3 shallots, finely chopped

olive oil

6 cups stock, vegetable or chicken

1 small glass wine

pinch of nutmeg, freshly grated

1 bay leaf

salt and finely ground pepper

grated gruyère cheese

toasted slices of French loaf

Fry the bacon with the shallots in a little olive oil and cook until the shallots are soft. Add the leeks and continue cooking until sweated. Do not allow the leeks to stick.

•

Add chicken stock, white wine, nutmeg, bay leaf and seasonings. Bring the stock to the boil, reduce the flame and simmer for 15 minutes. Check the seasoning.

•

Put the soup into deep soup bowls, put a piece of toast on top and cover with grated gruyère cheese. Put the soup bowls under a hot grill to brown the cheese. Serve at once.

Thai Fisherman's Soup

Peel the prawns, fry the shells in the peanut oil until they are pink. Add the chicken stock and the lemon grass cut into 1cm/½in lengths, kaffir leaves, lime peel and green chilli. Bring to the boil and simmer for 20 minutes. Strain through a fine sieve and bring to the boil again.

•

Cut the white meat of the scallops in half, leaving the coral attached to one half.

•

Add the prawns, mussels and scallops to the stock and cook for 2–3 minutes. Lower the heat and add the juice of the limes and the nam pla. Remove from the heat and serve decorated with the strips of kaffir leaf, sliced chilli and finely sliced lemon grass.

SERVES 8

900g/2lb raw Dublin Bay prawns

8 scallops

16 mussels

2 tablespoons peanut oil

2½ litres/4pt light chicken stock

3 stalks lemon grass, bruised

4 kaffir lime leaves, bruised

1 teaspoon julienne of lime peel

1 green chilli, finely sliced

2 large limes

1 tablespoon nam pla (fish sauce, page 25)

Garnish

1 kaffir lime leaf cut into thread julienne

1 small red chilli, sliced

1 stalk lemon grass, remove the tough outer layers and finely slice the tender parts

Aubergines in Carrozza
MELANZANE IN CARROZZA

SERVES 4

2 fat round purple aubergines weighing about 400g/14oz

175g/6oz buffalo mozzarella cheese

dried oregano

4 sun-dried tomatoes preserved in olive oil, about 60g/2oz

flour

2 eggs, beaten

Japanese breadcrumbs (page 24)

salt and freshly ground black pepper

olive oil

pizzaiola sauce (opposite)

If buffalo mozzarella is not available use cow's milk mozzarella instead. Ordinary dried breadcrumbs can be used instead of Japanese.

●

Cut the aubergines in $\frac{3}{4}$cm/$\frac{1}{4}$in slices, sprinkle with salt and leave them to drain in a colander for 1 hour.

●

Dry thoroughly, then grill the slices on a ridged griddle. Leave to cool.

●

Place slices of mozzarella between 2 slices of aubergine to make a sandwich, sprinkle oregano on top of the cheese and two slivers of dried tomato. Dip the aubergine sandwiches in flour, then in seasoned egg and finally in Japanese breadcrumbs.

●

Deep-fry the aubergines in light olive oil. Serve with pizzaiola sauce (opposite).

●

AUBERGINES *Preferably make sure that the aubergines you use look shiny and tight in their skins and have a heavy feel to them. Try to find the long narrow ones or the round ones: they seem to have less pappy centres than the pear-shaped variety.*

Pizzaiola Sauce

Fry the garlic in 2 tablespoons of extra-virgin olive oil, add the tomatoes, oregano, salt and freshly ground black pepper. Stir fry for 2 minutes; do not allow the tomatoes to become a pulp. We serve this sauce with melanzane in carrozza.

•

Pizzaiola sauce is usually served with a fettina of steak, a very thin slice of rump steak, preferably cooked on a charcoal grill.

SERVES 4–6

750g/1½lb plum tomatoes, peeled and chopped

2 cloves garlic, finely chopped

good pinch of dried oregano

extra-virgin olive oil

salt and freshly ground black pepper

Asparagus Gratinée

ASPARAGI ALLA PARMIGIANA

Wash the asparagus thoroughly, trim the stems removing the tough part. Bring a large pan of salted water to the boil. If you have a steamer, steam the asparagus. If not, boil the asparagus for 15 minutes; it is done when it is easily pierced with a fork. Drain on linen cloths.

•

Butter 4 gratin dishes, put in the asparagus, tips all facing one way. Season with salt.

•

Sprinkle the Parmesan on top of the asparagus and dot with the remaining unsalted butter. Bake in a hot oven, 450°F/230°C/gas 8; or grill for a few minutes until a light crust has formed on top of the asparagus. Remove from the oven, grind black pepper on top and serve at once.

•

Extra-virgin olive oil can replace the butter.

SERVES 4

1kg/2¼lb asparagus

150g/5oz unsalted butter

100g/3½oz freshly grated Parmesan cheese

salt and pepper

Stuffed Fried Zucchini Flowers
FIORI DI ZUCCHINI RIPIENI E FRITTI

SERVES 4

Stuffing

8 zucchini flowers with small zucchini attached

100g/3½oz ricotta

100g/3½oz mozzarella

40g/1¼oz freshly grated Parmesan cheese

30g/1oz finely chopped Parma ham (vegetarians can omit the ham and replace with 30g/1oz cooked spinach, finely chopped)

pinch of freshly grated nutmeg

salt and freshly ground black pepper

light olive oil for frying

Batter

200g/7oz self-raising wheatmeal flour

pinch of salt

2 cups iced water

Mix all the cheeses, Parma ham (spinach for the vegetarian version), and seasonings together. Divide the mixture into eight. Fill each flower with the stuffing. Just above the stuffing twist the flower petals slightly to keep the stuffing in.

•

The batter should be prepared just before you need it. Sift the flour, add the salt and iced water. The flour should be barely mixed with the water, the batter should look lumpy—do not worry if unmixed flour shows, this is correct.

•

Dip each flower into the batter. Deep-fry the flowers, until golden, in light olive oil. Drain on absorbent kitchen paper. Serve very hot.

Piedmontese Peppers
PEPERONI ALLA PIEDMONTESE

If anchovies are omitted this dish is suitable for vegetarians.

•

Wash the peppers, cut in half, de-seed and remove the white vein. Place the peppers on a baking tray. Put half a plum tomato in each half of the pepper and top with an anchovy fillet. Scatter the garlic and freshly ground pepper, very little salt is needed as the anchovies are already salty. Liberally sprinkle the extra-virgin olive oil over the peppers.

•

Cook in the oven set at 190°C/375°F/gas 5 for about 20 minutes, or until al dente.

•

Serve hot or cold with plenty of rough Italian-type bread.

•

This recipe is based on one from Elizabeth David's classic book, Italian Food, *written in 1954. We had this recipe on our first menu. Peppers were still hard to obtain in the UK in 1963, but we had a local supplier called Vin Sullivan, who managed to get them for us. This dish is still very popular at the restaurant, despite the fact that peppers are no longer a novelty.*

SERVES 4

2 red peppers

2 green peppers

4 fresh plum tomatoes, peeled

8 anchovy fillets

2 cloves garlic, finely chopped

freshly ground pepper

a little salt

90ml/3fl oz extra-virgin olive oil

DEEP-FRIED LAVER SEAWEED

SERVES 4

115g/4oz laver seaweed

flour

vegetable oil for deep-frying

roasted Schezuan pepper (see method)

salt

Wash the laver seaweed thoroughly. You will have to wash it many times to remove the sand, which adheres to it. Leave the seaweed to drain in a colander and then dry thoroughly. Tear the laver into strips, dip it in flour and shake off the excess.

•

Deep-fry the laver until crisp, about 2–3 minutes. Sprinkle with ground roasted Schezuan pepper and salt. Serve as a nibble with drinks.

•

To make roasted Schezuan pepper, dry fry the pepper until a strong aromatic perfume is given off, then grind in a spice grinder. A spice grinder is an absolute must in the kitchen as previously ground spices do not have the same aroma and taste.

•

LAVERBREAD *In Wales a tremendous amount of laver seaweed is eaten. Generally the laver is made into laverbread. A dish of laverbread consists of seaweed boiled to a mush, so it is rather a misnomer. The laverbread is mixed with oatmeal and made into small cakes, then fried in bacon fat and served with home-cured bacon.*

Olive Ascolane

Filling

600g/1lb 5oz Ascoli olives (large green olives)

100g/3½oz chicken breast

100g/3½oz pork

100g/3½oz veal

1 large tablespoon tomato passato

½ glass dry white wine

60g/2oz Parma ham, chopped

1 egg, beaten

1 thick slice bread, made into breadcrumbs

100g/3½oz freshly grated Parmesan cheese

pinch of nutmeg

pinch of cinnamon

grated rind of 1 lemon

1 tablespoon finely chopped parsley

salt and freshly ground black pepper

flour

2 eggs, beaten

dry breadcrumbs

lemon wedges

olive oil

The name Ascolane derives from the town of Ascoli Piceno (Marche). Ascoli was the ancient capital of the Piceni tribe, it lies in a narrow valley at the confluence of the rivers Castellano and Tronto, with the Sibillini mountains rising behind.

In the culinary world Ascoli is particularly renowned for its large green olives, which are made into the wonderfully appetising dish of olive ascolane. *The olives are stoned and stuffed with a mixture of meats and spices, dipped in breadcrumbs and deep-fried. They are fiddly to make but well worth it. These olives are also part of a* fritto misto ascolano *(page 134).*

•

Chop the chicken, pork and veal roughly and fry in 4 tablespoons of olive oil, until browned. Add the tomato passato and wine. Cook on a low heat until the meat is cooked, about 5 minutes, transfer the mixture with the Parma ham into a food processor and chop very finely. Put the mixture into a bowl, add one beaten egg, the fresh breadcrumbs, Parmesan, cinnamon, nutmeg, grated lemon peel, parsley, salt and pepper. Mix well.

•

Remove the stones from the olives by cutting round the stone with a sharp knife but keeping the olive in 1 piece. Stuff the olives with the mixture.

•

Roll the stuffed olives in flour, coat in the beaten egg and then in breadcrumbs. Deep-fry in hot light olive oil. Drain the olives on absorbent paper. Serve hot with lemon wedges, to accompany drinks.

FRIED CUSTARD
CREMA FRITTA

75g/2½oz sugar

90g/3oz plain flour

½ litre/¾ pt milk

a piece of vanilla pod

peel of 1 lemon

2 whole eggs

2 eggs, beaten

light olive oil for frying

golden dried breadcrumbs

Put the sugar and the flour in a saucepan. Bring the milk to the boil with the vanilla pod and lemon peel. Add the milk to the sugar and flour a little at a time, stirring all the time. Place the pan on the heat and continue stirring for 5 minutes. Remove the pan from the heat and add the whole eggs one at a time, return to the heat and cook, stirring constantly for another 5 minutes. Dampen a tray and pour the strained mixture to a depth of 2cm/1in; leave to go cold.

•

When the custard is completely cold, cut into 2½cm/1½in wide strips and then into 2½cm/1½in squares. Dip each square in beaten egg and then in breadcrumbs. Heat the olive oil and deep-fry until golden brown and crisp. Drain and serve as part of a fritto misto (page 134).

Crêpes Ile de France

SERVES 12 AS A STARTER
6 AS A MAIN COURSE

12 pancakes (method on page 50, omitting the laverbread)

115g/4oz butter

115g/4oz white cultivated mushrooms sliced

300ml/½pt milk

1 medium onion stuck with 2 cloves

1 bay leaf

30g/1oz flour

salt and freshly ground black pepper

12 thin slices cooked ham

2 tablespoons grated gruyère

2 tablespoons grated Parmesan cheese

Heat 30g/1oz butter in a frying pan, add the sliced mushrooms and sauté briskly for a minute or two.

•

Heat to boiling point the milk with the onion stuck with cloves and the bay leaf and leave to infuse for 15 minutes.

•

Melt 30g/1oz butter in a pan, stir in the flour and mix well, beat in the strained hot milk and cook for 5 minutes, stirring constantly until the mixture is smooth and thick. Fold in the mushrooms and any pan juices. Season with salt and freshly ground black pepper.

•

To assemble, place a slice of ham on each pancake, divide the mushroom mixture between the pancakes and loosely roll up. Place in a buttered gratin dish, dot with butter and sprinkle with grated gruyère and Parmesan cheese. Bake for 15 minutes in a hot oven 230°C/450°F/gas 8.

SEAFOOD PANCAKES
CRÊPES FRUITS DE MER

SERVES 12 AS A STARTER
6 AS A MAIN COURSE

Savoury pancakes

115g/4oz plain flour

pinch of salt

1 beaten egg

300ml/½pt milk

2 tablespoons laverbread

2 teaspoons olive oil

butter

Seafood filling

4 tablespoons finely chopped shallots

2 tablespoons butter

2 tablespoons plain flour

600ml/1pt warm milk

salt and freshly ground white pepper

pinch of freshly grated nutmeg

pinch of cayenne

2 tablespoons finely chopped parsley

To make the pancakes. Sift the flour and salt into a bowl, make a well in the centre, add the beaten egg and then gradually add the milk, stirring all the time. When the batter is free from lumps add the olive oil. Strain the batter through a fine sieve and stir in the laverbread. Leave the batter to stand for 2 hours. It should be as thin as single cream. Add a little more milk if the batter is too thick.

•

For each pancake, spoon about 2 tablespoons of batter onto a buttered crêpe pan, swirling the pan to allow the batter to cover the surface of the pan. (A heavy cast-iron crêpe pan is the best.) Cook over medium heat until golden and then flip over with a spatula and cook the other side. Layer the pancakes up between greaseproof paper so that they do not stick.

•

To make the seafood filling. In a saucepan, sauté the shallots in butter until transparent, sprinkle with flour and continue to cook, stirring constantly for 2–3 minutes. Add the warmed milk, salt, pepper, nutmeg, cayenne, parsley and bay leaf and using a wooden spoon stir until well blended. Add the double cream and wine and cook gently for a further 10 minutes, stirring occasionally. Stir in the seafood and heat through. Lay out 12 pancakes on a work table and put 2 heaped tablespoons of the seafood filling on each pancake, loosely roll them up and place in individual gratin dishes or 1 large one. Top with the remaining sauce and sprinkle with grated gruyère cheese and grated Parmesan cheese. Bake in a hot oven 230°C/450°F/gas 8 until golden brown. One pancake per person is ample for a first course, two for a main course.

1 bay leaf

2 tablespoons double cream

4 tablespoons white wine

450g/1lb mixed cooked seafood: prawns, mussels, small scallops, langoustine

2 tablespoons grated Parmesan cheese

2 tablespoons grated gruyère cheese

Cep and Walnut Salad

INSALATA DI PORCINI ALLE NOCI

SERVES 4

100g/3½oz mixed salad leaves, e.g. rocket, endive, young spinach leaves

8 walnuts, preferably fresh, new season (dried is acceptable)

200g/7oz ceps (porcini), they must be perfect specimens

100g/3½oz mature goat's cheese

julienne of 2 sticks of tender celery heart

extra-virgin olive oil

salt

Wash the salad leaves, dry them and divide them between 4 plates. Chop the nuts and mix them with 8 tablespoons of olive oil, season with salt. Slice the ceps very thinly and scatter them over the salad leaves. Dress the ceps with the walnut dressing. Shave the mature goat's cheese on top. Sprinkle julienne of celery over the salad.

Chicken of the Woods (Fungi) and Polenta

FUNGHI E POLENTA

SERVES 6

450g/1lb chicken of the woods (fungi)

6 shallots, finely chopped

3 cloves garlic, finely chopped

4 tablespoons extra-virgin olive oil

1 sprig thyme

2 tablespoons finely chopped parsley

salt and freshly ground black pepper

Clean and finely slice the fungi.

•

Fry the shallots and garlic in extra-virgin olive oil until golden, add the fungi and herbs and fry gently. Do not overcook or the fungi will break up. Season with salt and pepper.

•

Serve with grilled polenta (page 99) or a slice of toasted bread.

We have three spots which have become firm favourites for our mushroom gathering forays, and each spot has a breathtaking beauty. Our most prolific area is a wood in the Black Mountains. The terrain is difficult but the beauty of that wood and the baskets of porcini, chanterelles, pieds de mouton and trompettes de mort more than compensate for the aching limbs and sore back. The smell of the birch trees, the vast variety of mosses, the sun slanting through the branches in little patches, the sound of the waterfalls gushing down to the brook below and the smell of the mushrooms transport one away.

The yelps of excitement echo through the woods as the first mushrooms are sighted, then silence as the collecting gets more intense, then more yelps— someone has found a perfect specimen. Miles are covered without even being noticed. Baskets filled, we come down the wooded mountainside, staggering under their weight.

The forestry workers call out, "You've been picking those weird toadstools again have you?" We laugh, we can never convince them that those toadstools are delicious to eat.

It should be mentioned that mushrooms are very difficult for the human organism to digest so do not overdo the amount you eat. Mushrooms are not so much eaten for their nutritional value as for their flavour and smell. It is wise for people who suffer from digestive and liver problems—young children and the older generation who are frail—to avoid eating too many mushrooms.

GRATIN OF OYSTERS WITH LAVERBREAD

SERVES 4

24 oysters

100g/3½oz butter

1 small very finely chopped onion

1 tablespoon finely chopped parsley

juice ½ lemon

salt and freshly ground white pepper

200g/7oz laverbread

60g/2oz fresh fine white breadcrumbs

Open the oysters reserving half their juice, discarding the rest, and place them in the deepest shell halves. Discard the shallow halves. Mix together the butter, onion, parsley, lemon juice and the oyster juice. Season with salt and pepper. Spread the mixture over half the oysters, and cover the other half with laverbread.

•

Sprinkle with the breadcrumbs and cook in the oven 180°C/350°F/gas 4 for 4 minutes. Serve at once.

THAI MUSSELS

SERVES 4
AS A FIRST COURSE

1.8kg/4lb mussels

8 cloves garlic

1 large red chilli

2 tablespoons peanut oil

2 tablespoons nam pla (fish sauce, page 25)

a small bunch of chopped mint

Scrub the mussels well and remove the beards (remove any broken or open mussels). Chop the garlic and the chilli finely. Heat the peanut oil in a frying pan and fry the garlic and chilli mixture until golden. Add the nam pla followed by the mussels. Cover. When the mussels have opened (this will take only a few minutes), discard half of the shells, place the remaining shells on a serving dish. Do not use any mussels that have not opened properly. Add the mint to the mussel juice and pour over the mussels.

•

This dish was taught to us by a young Thai chef who came to stay one weekend. He said it was his Thai version of Moules Marinière. The flavours of this dish are so exciting we decided to put it on the menu.

ANTIPASTO DI MARE

SUGGESTED DISHES FOR ANTIPASTO DI MARE

Mussels pescatora *(page 58)*

Capesante alla marinara *(page 185)*

Calamaretti con olio e aglio *(page 184)*

Scampi alla griglia *(page 187)*

Cockles in potacchio *(page 59)*

Antipasto di mare is found on the menu of every fish restaurant along the Marche's Adriatic coast. What could be more pleasant than sitting on a terrace overlooking the sea eating antipasto di mare, mopping up the oil and garlic juices from the shellfish with the local unsalted bread and washing it all down with a glass of chilled local white Verdicchio wine. The antipasto di mare very much depends on the catch of the day. Sometimes sea snails (imporchetta) are added, vongole marinara instead of mussels and so on. Although The Walnut Tree is not by the sea, shellfish for this dish are delivered from the coast every morning and although the customers have mountains to look out at, not the sea, it is nevertheless a very popular dish.

PEPPER MUSSELS
COZZE IMPEPATE

Clean the mussels; remove the beards and scrub well. Discard any that are damaged or broken.

•

In a large pan fry the garlic in the olive oil, add the wine and reduce by four-fifths. Add the mussels and the peppercorns. Remove the pan from the heat as soon as the mussels are open.

•

Serve the mussels with parsley sprinkled on top. A mixture of mussels and clams can be used for this dish. A concassé (small dice of fruit or vegetables) of lemon is also good scattered on top of the mussels.

SERVES 4

1.6kg/3½lb mussels

2 cloves garlic, finely chopped

60ml/2fl oz extra-virgin olive oil

1 generous glass dry white wine

fresh green peppercorns (approx. 1 tablespoon), lightly crushed

2 tablespoons finely chopped parsley

LEMON VINAIGRETTE

Blend all the ingredients together with a fork. Chopped herbs such as parsley and chives can be added to this dressing, which is very good on prawns, crab or monkfish and also on cold vegetables or on a green salad.

In Italy lemons are considered to have antiseptic properties. During the hot summer months in the Marche, lemon juice is poured liberally over fish and shellfish hopefully to kill off any lurking bacteria. About twenty years

juice of 1 large lemon

4 tablespoons extra-virgin olive oil

pinch of sea salt

pinch of freshly ground black pepper

ago, when there was a cholera scare in Italy, lemons suddenly became very hard to get as people were encouraged to drink the pure juice and put it on their food. Vans with loudspeakers toured the towns and villages advising people not to eat fish and to drink wine or lemon juice either pure or with mineral water added—wine with a medical blessing!

Mussels Pescatora

SERVES 4

400g/14oz per person fresh mussels, well washed and beard removed

3 cloves garlic, finely chopped (optional)

2 tablespoons chopped parsley

juice of 1 lemon

3 tablespoons extra-virgin oil

freshly ground black pepper

lemon wedges

In a large pan, fry the garlic briefly in the extra-virgin olive oil. Add the mussels, parsley, lemon juice and pepper. Cook the mussels covered over a brisk heat, stirring them occasionally. When the mussels have opened, remove them with a perforated spoon. Pour the sauce over the mussels and serve hot with lemon wedges and plenty of bread to mop up the juices. If omitting the garlic, put the mussels in a large pan and add the oil, lemon juice, finely chopped parsley and pepper. Cook for 7–8 minutes or until the mussels open.

Vongole or Cockles in Potacchio
VONGOLE IN POTACCHIO

Purge the vongole or cockles (page 77). Put the vongole or cockles to boil with the wine. When they are open drain them, strain and reserve the liquor. Reject half the shells and rinse the cockles to remove any remaining sand. Fry the garlic, rosemary and half the fennel until the garlic is golden. Add the tomato paste and fry until shiny, pour in the reserved cooking liquor. Let the sauce cook until it gets to a thick consistency. Add the cockles to the sauce, season with salt, pepper and chilli to taste, stir in the remaining fennel. Serve as part of an antipasto di mare.

SERVES 8

2kg/4½lb vongole or cockles in their shells

4 cloves garlic, finely chopped

1 tablespoon finely chopped fresh rosemary

8 tablespoons finely chopped fresh fennel

250g/½lb tomato paste

125ml/4fl oz dry white wine

6 tablespoons extra-virgin olive oil

pinch of chilli flakes

salt and freshly ground black pepper

Spinach Tart

SERVES 8

__Filling__

350g/12oz lightly cooked fresh spinach, roughly chopped

2 tablespoons olive oil

salt and freshly ground black pepper

1 pinch ground chilli

1 teaspoon finely chopped garlic

225g/8oz ricotta

3 eggs, lightly beaten

60g/2oz freshly grated Parmesan cheese

6 tablespoons double cream

freshly grated nutmeg to taste

__Pastry__

225g/8oz plain flour

pinch of salt

1 level tablespoon icing sugar

150g/5oz softened butter

1 egg

To make the pastry. Sieve flour, salt and sugar into a bowl, rub in the butter until mixture resembles breadcrumbs. Use your hands lightly. Beat the egg and add chilled water, sprinkle over dough and work in lightly with your fingertips. Leave the dough in a refrigerator for 1 hour. Roll out and line a 25cm/10in loose-bottomed quiche tin, prick the base with a fork and bake blind in a hot oven 220°C/425°F/gas 7 for about 15 minutes. Allow to cool.

•

Heat the oil in a frying pan, add the spinach and toss. Season with salt, pepper, chilli and garlic, remove from the heat. Add the ricotta cheese, beaten eggs, Parmesan cheese, double cream and nutmeg to taste, mix in well. Spread mixture in pastry shell and bake in moderate oven 180°C/350°F/gas 4 for 30 minutes, or until the crust is brown and the cheese mixture set.

•

Cicoria catalagna *(a type of cultivated dandelion) or wild hop shoots can be used instead of spinach.*

ZUCCHINI QUICHE

Make the pastry and leave in a refrigerator for 30 minutes.

•

Meanwhile, toss the zucchini in oil with a walnut of butter, add the garlic, salt and spices and toss until the zucchini are al dente. They must not be floppy. Drain onto kitchen paper. In a bowl, amalgamate the eggs and cheeses, season, then add the cream.

•

Heat the oven to 190°C/375°F/gas 5. Roll out the pastry, line a 25cm/10in loose-bottomed quiche tin, and bake blind on the middle shelf for about 15 minutes.

•

Then scatter the zucchini over the pastry and cover with the egg and cream mixture. Cook the quiche for another 30 minutes. Serve tepid.

SERVES 8

Pastry

200g/7oz plain flour

130g/4½oz butter

6 tablespoons iced water

pinch of salt

Filling

500g/1lb 2oz zucchini, thinly sliced

butter

5 whole eggs

500ml/16fl oz single cream

20g/¾oz grated Emmental

90g/3oz grated Parmesan cheese

6 tablespoons extra-virgin olive oil

salt and pepper to taste

pinch of roasted Szechuan pepper

pinch of chilli pepper

1 clove garlic, finely chopped

Lady Llanover's Salt Duck

For this dish use only the breast of duck left on the bone. Weigh the duck breasts and for every 2.8kg/6lb of duck meat and carcass rub in 225g/8oz of coarse sea salt. The duck should be placed in a deep container, breast-side down. Keep in a cool place. After 1½ days turn the breasts over. After 3 days rinse off the salt, place the duck breasts in a deep oven dish and stand it in a baking tray. Cover the duck with cold water and also put water in the baking tray. Place the tray in the centre of an oven set at 160°C/300°F/gas 2 and cook uncovered for 1½ hours. Remove the duck breasts from the liquid and leave to cool. Serve the duck breast thinly sliced with gooseberry pickle, crab apple and rowanberry jelly (both on page 64) and pickled damsons (opposite).

August Hall, Lady Llanover, wife of Benjamin Hall, later Baron Llanover of Big Ben fame, lived at Llanover Court near Abergavenny.

She was a very influential figure in Welsh cultural life during the 19th century. She promoted the Welsh language, literature, costume and also the Eisteddfod. One of the deeds she is very much remembered for round here is that she closed all the pubs in Llanover!

Lady Llanover published her cookery book The First Principles of Good Cookery *in 1867. In 1991 a facsimile was published. Bobby Freeman wrote the introduction to the book, explaining its significance in the history of cooking and the background of Lady Llanover's life. Bobby asked us to arrange a menu culled from the book for its launch. The first course we devised, with the help of Elizabeth David, was Lady Llanover's salt duck.*

PICKLED DAMSONS

4 litres/7pt damsons

1.8kg/4lb preserving sugar

450ml/¾pt red wine vinegar

1 10cm/4in stick cinnamon

6 cloves

Wash and prick the damsons with a silver fork. Make a syrup from the sugar and vinegar. Put the damsons in the syrup and bring the syrup back to the boil. Remove the damsons quickly at this point, with a perforated spoon, and lay them on flat trays to quickly cool. Add the spices to the syrup and boil for a further 5–10 minutes or until the syrup thickens again. Put the fruit carefully into sterilized glass jars, strain the syrup over the fruit while it is still hot. Cover while still hot. Keeping time? Until next crop. Good served with Lady Llanover's salt duck.

Crab Apple and Rowanberry Jelly

750g/1½lb crab apples

750g/1½lb rowanberries

1.8 litre/3pt water

jam sugar

Wash the fruits well, put them in a preserving pan with the water, bring to the boil and boil until the fruit is very soft. Strain the fruit and liquid through a jelly bag. To every pint of liquid add 1lb of jam sugar. Return the liquid to the heat, add the sugar. Bring slowly to the boil, stirring continuously until the sugar has dissolved, then boil fast until the liquid jells when dripped onto a saucer. It will wrinkle when it is ready. Pour the jelly into warm sterilized dry jars, cover with circles of waxed paper while hot, then cover with cellophane circles when cold.

Gooseberry Pickle

450g/1lb gooseberries (underripe)

300ml/½pt white wine vinegar

60g/2oz sugar

pinch of ground ginger

2½cm/1in stick cinnamon

6 cloves

Top and tail the gooseberries. Make a syrup from the white wine vinegar and sugar with the ground ginger, the piece of cinnamon and cloves added. Poach the gooseberries very briefly in the syrup. Remove the gooseberries and place in hot sterilized jars. Pour the syrup over the gooseberries when cold. Leave for a few weeks before using.

•

When serving, sprinkle a little julienne of fresh ginger on top of the gooseberries.

•

Slightly underripe gooseberries are best for this pickle. It will keep until the following season.

Bresoala

We learned this recipe from a restaurant called Piperno in the Jewish quarter in Rome. The owner very kindly gave us the recipe and demonstrated the method.

•

Trim the joint of beef, removing fat and sinews.

•

Put all the ingredients for the marinade in a large bowl, add the meat, cover and leave for 1 week in a cool place or until the meat feels firm.

•

Hang the meat in a dry, airy place for another week until it feels firm enough to be sliced thinly. It will feel solid, no give at all as you press with your fingers. Rub the joint with olive oil, wrap in greaseproof paper and keep in the refrigerator until required.

•

To serve, slice very thinly. Sprinkle with olive oil and season with pepper and chives. Garnish with wedges of lemon.

•

Do not attempt to preserve a smaller piece of meat, it is not satisfactory. Bresoala, like Parma ham, has a long life and keeps well for 3 months.

4kg/9lb topside beef (after trimming)

extra-virgin olive oil

fresh roughly ground black pepper

chopped chives

Marinade

enough red and white wine to cover the joint (equal amounts)

750g/1¾lb coarse sea salt

a large bunch of rosemary

12 bay leaves

24 cloves

3 cloves garlic, crushed

40 black peppercorns

12 dried chillies

4 strips orange peel

RAW FILLET OF BEEF AND TRUFFLES
CARPACCIO "ST ANGELO IN VADO"

SERVES 4

a selection of small, tender salad greens: endive, oak leaf, rocket, frisée, batavia, radicchio

vinaigrette dressing

wafer-thin slices of raw beef fillet (chill the meat and slice on a meat slicer, which is preferable, or with a very sharp knife)

shavings of Parmesan cheese (use potato-peeler)

thin shavings of white truffle

Dress the salad leaves lightly with vinaigrette. Divide the leaves between four dinner plates. Season the wafer thin slices of beef with salt and pepper. Gently arrange 45g/1½oz beef on each plate. Scatter Parmesan shavings and truffle shavings on top. Serve immediately.

We had gone together with our then small daughter to a village called St Angelo in Vado up in the mountains of the Marche region. It is a village famous for its truffles. The whole place is pervaded by the smell of truffles during the season.

Our daughter had been somewhat bored by this trip and as we were discussing the price of truffles in the piazza with one of the cerca tartufi *(truffle hunters) she wandered off to peer into a brightly lit window below ground level. After a few minutes she came back and pulled us over to the window. There we watched a cook in a kitchen preparing what we have called Carpaccio St Angelo in Vado.*

It is from this village that Franco learned to use truffles with such abandon. He always says as he shaves them over food, "Let the customers enjoy them, never mind the profit."

Bavarois of Smoked Salmon

This recipe is based on a bavarois of smoked salmon we once ate at a restaurant called Chiberta in Paris. I have given the recipe for 10 people because it is a dish which can be served at a dinner party without stress to the cook.

•

Rinse 10 ramekins with cold water, do not dry. Line the ramekins with thin slices of smoked salmon, leaving a little salmon to fold over and trim off any excess that overhangs too much.

•

Blend the remaining salmon and trimmings in a food processor with the crème fraîche, cayenne and lemon juice until smooth. Fold in the caviar very gently. Divide the mixture between the ramekins. Gently fold over the overhanging salmon. Cover with a piece of greaseproof paper, then a sheet of foil. Refrigerate until ready to use.

•

To make the tomato coulis. Fry the shallots in a little olive oil until golden. Add the tomatoes and stir fry until well cooked. Season with salt and freshly ground black pepper. Sieve the tomatoes and leave to get cold, then refrigerate. To serve, make a puddle of tomato coulis on a plate, tip a bavarois on top and sprinkle with chopped chives.

SERVES 10

Bavarois

750g/1½lb smoked salmon, thinly sliced

1 cup crème fraîche

½ teaspoon cayenne pepper

juice of ½ lemon

8 teaspoons red caviar

Tomato coulis

900g/2lb plum or very ripe ordinary tomatoes, quartered

2 tablespoons finely chopped shallots

salt and pepper

olive oil

Garnish

chopped chives

Foccacia with Olive, Onion and Rosemary

FOCCACIA CON OLIVE, CIPOLLE E ROSMARINO

900g/2lb flour

salt

60g/2oz fresh yeast

sugar

350ml/12fl oz warm water

150ml/¼pt extra-virgin olive oil, plus 6 tablespoons

150ml/¼pt dry white wine

rosemary

slivers of onion

400g/14oz stoned black olives, halved

coarse sea salt

Put the flour and salt in a bowl and make a well. Dissolve the yeast in a ½ glass water, adding a pinch of sugar. Leave to froth.

•

Stir the yeast into the flour. Stir in the oil and wine, then add the rest of the water. Knead for 10–15 minutes, adding a little flour if it is too sticky. Then add two-thirds of the stoned olives. Leave the dough to rise in a warm draught-free place for 1–2 hours, covered with a cloth.

•

Punch the dough down and knead for 1–2 minutes. Roll out the dough into 3 oblongs: 25×38×1cm/10×15×½in. Sprinkle generously with sea salt and the rest of the olives. Press in little sprigs of rosemary and thin slivers of onion. Make depressions with your thumb all over the dough. Bake in a very hot oven (250°C/475°F/gas 9) for 25 minutes. Eat hot, sprinkled with extra-virgin olive oil.

Walnut Bread

Mix the flour, sugar, salt, melted butter and olive oil together. Dissolve the yeast in the milk. Add the milk and yeast to the flour mixture. Add the carbonated water.

●

Knead the mixture until a smooth dough is obtained. Leave the dough to rise for $1\frac{1}{2}$ hours. Knead the dough briefly and cut into 8 pieces. Pass each piece of dough through a pasta machine until an oblong is obtained, about $1\frac{1}{2}$cm/$\frac{1}{2}$in thick.

●

Spread each oblong with roughly broken walnuts and roll up. Place the rolls in hovis tins and leave to rise for 1 hour. Brush the dough with egg wash and bake for 30 minutes in an oven set at 190°C/375°F/gas 5. Place on the middle shelf.

●

This bread can be made with different fillings, such as chopped olives, olive paste, dried tomato paste, garlic and rosemary. It may seem a lot of bread to make but it freezes well.

MAKES 8 LOAVES

3kg/$6\frac{1}{2}$lb Farina O flour

45g/$1\frac{1}{2}$oz sugar

50g/$1\frac{3}{4}$oz salt

250g/$\frac{1}{2}$lb melted butter

1 glass extra-virgin olive oil

200g/7oz yeast

650ml/$1\frac{1}{4}$pt milk

carbonated mineral water

400g/1lb walnuts, roughly chopped

egg wash

Sei
Colli

Pasta, Risottos and Polenta

Pasta is the common denominator between the cooking of the coastal, country and mountain regions of the Marche. The pasta is made from hard wheat flour, with sauces made from fish, game, vegetables and truffles.

When we first came to The Walnut Tree we made the pasta by hand. I (Franco) used to go to my mother-in-law's house to make the pasta; my mother-in-law and I would spend hours making pasta, hanging it from a Victorian clothes drier to dry. Come to think of it, I think we only bought a hand machine because she got rid of the drier. The hand machines were brought out every day first thing in the morning by the two Italian ladies who started to work for us. Now we have a large electric machine which churns out all the shapes and sizes one could possibly wish for. There is still not a machine that makes pasta quite as perfectly as by hand. To eat pasta made by hand is a revelation.

Despite what I have written regarding pasta, if you do not feel like making it either by hand or with a hand machine, do not be put off. Buy dry pasta, there are many excellent brands available in this country these days. Also some of the fresh pasta shops turn out a passable pasta.

To make pasta using a hand machine

When we make pasta with a hand machine or entirely by hand we use Farina O. This flour is obtainable in Italian delicatessens. If this flour is unobtainable, use strong white flour instead. Farina OO is better for electric pasta machines.

•

Put the flour in a mound on a work surface, make a hollow. Add a little salt to the eggs, beat lightly with a fork and pour into the hollow. Draw the flour into the eggs until it is well amalgamated. If the mixture is too moist add a little more flour.

•

On a clean area of the work surface knead the dough with the heel of the palm of the hand, keeping your fingers bent, folding the pasta in half and giving it a half turn, keep doing this for 10 minutes. This process can be done in a food processor or, after the initial amalgamating together, the pasta can be rolled through the rollers of a pasta machine set at maximum width 4 or 5 times, or until the pasta is smooth. Thin the pasta progressively until the desired thickness is reached, according to the type of pasta you are making. Keep pasta not being rolled covered with clingfilm. As the pasta is done lay on clean teacloths in readiness for boiling.

•

Leave the pasta to dry for an hour before boiling.

HINTS ON COOKING PASTA

Use a pan that is deeper than it is wide.

•

Allow 1 litre/1¾pt of water for every 100g/3½oz of pasta, and 7g/¼oz salt for every litre/1¾pt.

•

Only put the pasta into the water when it is boiling hard.

•

Always stir the pasta frequently during cooking to avoid it sticking. Fresh pasta takes only a few minutes to cook—watch it carefully. Drain the pasta when it is *al dente*—firm but not crunchy to the bite. Do not drain too thoroughly, a little cooking water helps integrate sauce with pasta.

SPAGHETTI WITH GARLIC, OIL AND CHILLI

SPAGHETTI CON AGLIO, OLIO E PEPERONCINO

Boil the pasta in plenty of salted water until al dente. In a frying pan, gently heat the olive oil. Add the garlic and chilli, toss in the drained spaghetti and remove the pan from the heat. Toss in the parsley and serve at once.

SERVES 4

350g/12oz spaghetti

3 tablespoons extra-virgin olive oil

2 cloves garlic, finely chopped

1 red chilli pepper, finely chopped, or 1 good pinch dried chilli flakes

1 tablespoon finely chopped parsley

Spaghetti with Sun-dried Tomatoes, Garlic and Chilli

SPAGHETTI CON POMODORI SECCHI

SERVES 4

350g/12oz spaghetti

Sauce

12–14 sun-dried tomatoes in olive oil, cut in julienne

3 cloves garlic, finely chopped

good pinch of dried chilli flakes

salt and freshly ground black pepper

5 tablespoons extra-virgin olive oil

1 tablespoon finely chopped flatleaf parsley

Boil the spaghetti in abundant boiling salted water until al dente. Meanwhile, mix all the ingredients for the sauce together. When the spaghetti is almost ready, heat the tomato and oil mixture in a frying pan. Drain the spaghetti and toss it well into the tomato mixture. Serve at once.

Spaghetti with Truffle Paste and Zucchini Flowers

SPAGHETTI CON CREMA DI TARTUFO E FIORI DI ZUCCHINI

Pick zucchini flowers with a tiny zucchini no bigger than 5cm/2in long. Wash the flowers, remove the stamens and cut the vegetable part into thin slices leaving a tiny bit attached to the flower. Cut the flower into single petals. Melt the butter over a low flame and add the finely chopped garlic, zucchini flowers and zucchini slices. Cook gently for a few minutes; do not overcook them, they must still have a bite to them.

•

Stir in 4 tablespoons of truffle paste and add the spaghetti. Toss well in the sauce and season with salt and freshly ground white pepper. Serve at once with grated Parmesan. If you have a white truffle to shave on top, this would be magical.

SERVES 4

350g/12oz spaghetti, cooked al dente and drained

8 zucchini flowers

4 tablespoons truffle paste

1 clove garlic, finely chopped

100g/3½oz butter

salt and freshly ground white pepper

freshly grated Parmesan cheese

1 white truffle (optional)

Spaghetti with Lobster Sauce
SPAGHETTI CON SUGO DI AROGOSTA

SERVES 4

350g/12oz spaghetti

1 small lobster

250g/9oz plum tomatoes, peeled and finely chopped

1 clove garlic, finely chopped

1 bunch of fresh fennel fronds, finely chopped

2 tablespoons olive oil

salt and freshly ground black pepper

Boil the lobster for 5 minutes in boiling salted water. Remove the lobster from the pot and plunge it in cold water to cool. Extract the meat from the shell. Cut the meat into cubes.

•

Boil the spaghetti in plenty of boiling salted water until al dente. In a pan heat the olive oil. Add the garlic and fennel and fry briefly. Add the tomatoes and leave to cook for a few minutes, then add the lobster and heat through. Season with salt.

•

Serve sauce with the spaghetti and sprinkle freshly ground black pepper on top.

Spaghetti with Rosemary
SPAGHETTI CON ROSMARINO

SERVES 4

350g/12oz spaghetti

3 tablespoons extra-virgin olive oil

3 cloves garlic, finely chopped

½ handful tiny sprigs of rosemary

Boil the spaghetti in plenty of salted water, cook al dente. Gently warm the olive oil and add the garlic and rosemary. Strain the spaghetti and toss in the oil and herb mixture, season with salt.

•

Serve at once. If desired, Parmesan cheese can be served with this dish.

Spaghetti with Clam or Cockle Sauce

SPAGHETTI CON SUGO DI VONGOLE

SERVES 4

350g/12oz spaghetti

1 litre/1¾pt clams or cockles in shells

3 tablespoons extra-virgin olive oil

1 onion, finely chopped

4 cloves garlic, finely chopped

750g/1½lb ripe tomatoes, peeled, seeded and diced

1 glass white wine

1 generous pinch dried chilli flakes

4 tablespoons finely chopped flatleaf parsley

salt and freshly ground black pepper

Wash and purge the clams or cockles well: leave in a bucket of cold water with a handful of fine oatmeal stirred in for an hour or so.

•

Cook the shellfish in a saucepan without any water, stirring from time to time. When all the shells are open, strain and reserve the liquor. Remove the flesh from the shells. Fry the onion and garlic in the extra-virgin olive oil until soft but not coloured, add the parsley and quickly fry. Add the tomatoes and fry for a few minutes, add the white wine, then add the liquor from the shellfish. Season with salt and pepper and a generous pinch of chilli flakes, and reduce well. Add the clams or cockles, bring the sauce to the boil and remove the pan from the heat.

•

Serve as a sauce for spaghetti. Do not be tempted to serve Parmesan cheese.

•

If your tomatoes are not very ripe, stir-fry a half cupful of tomato purée in olive oil for a few minutes, and add this to the sauce.

AUBERGINE AND TOMATO SAUCE
SUGO DI POMODORO E MELANZANE

SERVES 4

wholewheat fettuccine (page 93)

100g/3½oz aubergine

300g/10oz ripe tomatoes, peeled, seeded and diced

1 medium onion

1 clove garlic, finely chopped

3 tablespoons extra-virgin olive oil

1 green chilli, seeded and finely chopped

3–4 basil leaves

40g/1½oz freshly grated pecorino or Parmesan cheese

salt and freshly ground black pepper

Tagliatelle originated from the region of Emilia-Romagna. Fettuccine are a Roman invention. They are interchangeable, the only difference being that fettuccine are slightly narrower.

•

Finely slice the aubergine and onion.

•

Fry the onion and garlic in the oil until soft and golden, then add the aubergine and chilli and cook over medium heat for 5 minutes. Add the tomatoes, peeled, seeded and diced, season with salt and pepper, and basil leaves torn up. Cook for a further 4 minutes.

•

Serve with wholewheat fettuccine and freshly grated pecorino or Parmesan cheese.

WIDE RIBBON NOODLES WITH HARE SAUCE
PAPPARDELLE CON SUGO DI LEPRE

Pappardelle are strips of pasta cut with a pastry cutter from a whole sheet of pasta. The strips should be 10–20cm/4–8in long by 2–3cm/¾–1¼in wide. Use the recipe for making tagliatelle on page 89 omitting the squid ink and cutting the pasta strips wider with a pastry cutter.

•

Marinate the hare in the wine and herbs for 24 hours at least.

•

Heat 3 tablespoons olive oil in a frying pan. Add the onion, celery, garlic and bacon. Fry until golden, remove with a perforated spoon to a casserole. Drain the pieces of hare, dry them and dust with flour. Add 4 tablespoons of olive oil to the existing oil in the frying pan, fry the pieces of hare until sealed, then add to the casserole. Heat the wine marinade and pour over the hare. Add a fresh bouquet garni. Season with salt and freshly ground black pepper.

•

Cover the casserole and gently cook the hare. The time greatly depends on the age of the hare, so check after 1 hour.

•

Remove pieces as they cook and remove the meat from the bone. Cut the meat into small pieces, return to the sauce and check the seasoning. The sauce should be thickish.

•

Serve with pappardelle and Parmesan.

SERVES 6

600g/1¼lb fresh pappardelle

1 hare, portioned

red wine, to cover the pieces

bouquet garni including rosemary

extra-virgin olive oil

1 onion, finely chopped

1 stalk celery, finely chopped

1 clove garlic, finely chopped

50g/2oz bacon, diced

flour for dusting

1 bouquet garni

salt and freshly ground black pepper

freshly grated Parmesan cheese

PAPPARDELLE WITH CEP SAUCE
PAPPARDELLE CON FUNGHI PORCINI

SERVES 4

600g/1¼lb fresh pappardelle (see page 79)

500g/1lb 2oz fresh porcini

20 walnut halves, chopped

1 clove garlic, finely chopped

½ glass dry white wine

1 bunch parsley, finely chopped

2 tablespoons extra-virgin olive oil

2 small ladles vegetable or meat stock

salt and freshly ground black pepper

Slice the mushrooms and fry them in 2 tablespoons of extra-virgin olive oil. Add the chopped garlic and parsley and fry briefly. Add the white wine, reduce the wine over a brisk flame, add the stock and leave to cook over a brisk flame until the stock is reduced to a glaze. Add the chopped walnuts and season with salt and pepper. Boil the pappardelle in plenty of boiling salted water until al dente. Drain the pasta. Pour the mushroom and walnut sauce over the pasta and sprinkle with freshly ground black pepper.

PAPPARDELLE WITH SCALLOPS AND PESTO
PAPPARDELLE CON CAPESANTE E SALSA DI PESTO

SERVES 4

Pasta

300g/10oz Farina O flour

3 large eggs

generous pinch of salt

Pesto

20 fresh basil leaves

20 flatleaf parsley leaves

3 cloves garlic

50g/2oz pine nuts

1 wine glass extra-virgin olive oil

salt and pepper to taste

Scallops

200g/7oz small scallops or large ones cut in half

2 tablespoons extra-virgin olive oil

4 tablespoons tomato concassé (peeled, seeded and diced tomato)

24 small sprigs fresh dill

olive oil

salt and pepper

Make the pasta in the usual way (page 72) and cut it into 2.5×7.5cm/1×3in strips with a pastry cutter.

•

Mix together all the ingredients for the pesto and process in a food processor until it is a paste.

•

Sauté the scallops in the olive oil and season with salt and pepper. Toss the scallops with 2 large tablespoons of pesto.

•

Cook the pasta until al dente, strain and toss with the scallops and pesto. Serve at once, decorated with tomato concassé and small sprigs of dill.

Pasta Envelopes with Pumpkin Filling and Walnut Sauce

RAVIOLI DI ZUCCA CON SALSA DI NOCE

SERVES 4–6

Filling

pumpkin, weighing about 900g/2lb before cleaning

175g/6oz freshly grated Parmesan cheese

½ teaspoon freshly grated nutmeg

salt and freshly ground white pepper

Pasta dough

450g/1lb Farina O flour

5 large eggs

pinch of salt

egg wash for sealing

Cut the pumpkin in half and remove the seeds and the stringy fibres. Place the halves cut-side down, on a baking tray and bake in a medium oven until soft, about 45 minutes. In a microwave, this takes about 10 minutes.

•

Remove the pumpkin from the heat and let it cool sufficiently to handle. Peel off the skin and leave the flesh to drain in a sieve for 1 hour. Purée the pumpkin in a food processor or mash with a fork. Leave to drain in a sieve to remove excess water. Add 115g/4oz of the Parmesan to the purée and the nutmeg, salt and pepper. Blend to a smooth consistency.

•

Knead the pasta dough ingredients together to make a pliable dough. Roll through a hand pasta machine as for lasagne, the last setting should be number 1. Cut into 10cm/4in squares.

•

To assemble the ravioli. Put a heaped teaspoon of the pumpkin mixture on one half of the square and fold over diagonally. Brush a little egg wash (beaten egg) round the edges of the pasta triangles to seal. This is a moist filling, so the envelopes cannot be kept too long.

•

Cook the pasta in plenty of salted boiling water. The ravioli will cook in a very short time, about 1 minute. When they rise to the top of the pan, check they are al dente, and drain.

•

Serve with walnut sauce (below) or melted butter with sage infused in it. Serve with extra Parmesan.

Walnut Sauce
SALSA DI NOCE

SERVES 4–6

24–30 walnut halves

2 cloves garlic, crushed

1 generous bunch parsley, finely chopped

1 pinch dried chilli flakes

175ml/6fl oz extra-virgin olive oil

salt and freshly ground black pepper to taste

Chop the walnuts finely *by hand.* A food processor is not suitable for this–it crushes the walnuts too much. Add the rest of the ingredients and mix together.

TAGLIATELLE WITH WHITE TRUFFLES
TAGLIATELLE CON TARTUFI BIANCHI

SERVES 4

Pasta

500g/1lb 2oz Farina O flour

4 eggs

pinch of salt

Sauce

truffle, preferably white

175g/6oz unsalted butter

8 tablespoons dry white wine

salt and freshly ground black pepper

2 pinches freshly grated nutmeg

4 tablespoons freshly grated Parmesan cheese

Make the pasta dough in the usual way (page 72). Pass the dough through the pasta machine three or four times; the final setting should be number 1. Then cut the sheets of pasta on the tagliatelle cutter of the machine.

•

In a small saucepan, melt the butter. Add the wine and reduce briskly by half. Season with salt, pepper and nutmeg.

•

Cook the pasta al dente, drain and toss the pasta in the sauce. Mix in the Parmesan. Serve with shaved truffle on top.

•

The more generous you are with the truffle the better the dish!

TAGLIATELLE WITH SEAFOOD
TAGLIATELLE ALLA MARINARA

SERVES 4

450g/1lb fresh tagliatelle (page 84)

750g/1½lb fresh mussels

750g/1½lb fresh cockles

350g/¾lb raw Dublin bay prawn tails, or prawns

2 small squid

1 small onion

2 cloves garlic

3 tablespoons extra-virgin olive oil

finely chopped parsley

1 glass dry white wine

pinch of ground chilli powder

salt and freshly ground black pepper

2 tablespoons finely chopped parsley

Clean and cook the mussels and cockles without any extra liquid. When they open, discard the shells and any that are unopened. Reserve the sieved cooking liquor.

•

Cook the prawns in salted boiling water. When the water starts to bubble again, strain and plunge into cold water. This stops the prawns from overcooking. Remove the shells.

•

Cut the squid into fine rings.

•

Finely chop the onion and garlic, and fry in the olive oil until golden. Add the squid and cook gently for a few minutes. Add the cooking liquor and wine and let it reduce over brisk heat until it forms a glaze. Add the rest of the shellfish, parsley, wine, chilli and pepper. Check if salt is necessary.

•

Cook the tagliatelle in abundant salted water until al dente. Strain, mix in the seafood sauce and sprinkle with finely chopped parsley. Serve at once.

Chestnut Tagliatelle
TAGLIATELLE DI CASTAGNE

SERVES 4–6

100g/3½oz chestnut flour

150g/5oz plain white flour

2 eggs

salt

Mix the two flours. Sieve the flours onto a work top, make a hollow in the middle, crack the eggs into the hollow, and add the salt. Mix all the ingredients together, adding a few drops of water if the mixture seems too dry.

•

Knead the dough until it is smooth and elastic. Put the dough in a polythene bag and leave it to rest in a fridge for half an hour.

•

Pass the dough through the pasta machine three or four times; the final setting should be number 1. Then cut the sheets of pasta on the tagliatelle cutter of the machine.

•

Boil the chestnut tagliatelle in plenty of boiling water until al dente.

•

Serve with game which has been cooked with a sauce, for example, Salmì of Hare (page 160).

BACCALÀ SAUCE
SALSA DI BACCALÀ

SERVES 4

500g/1lb baccalà (already soaked, page 191)

½ onion, finely chopped

12 cloves garlic, finely chopped

1 glass white wine

1½ litres/2½pt tomato coulis

1 tablespoon tomato purée

8 anchovy fillets, finely mashed

6 tablespoons extra-virgin olive oil

freshly ground black pepper

finely chopped parsley

Gently fry the garlic and onion in the olive oil, add 1 glass of dry white wine and allow it to bubble fiercely for a few minutes. Reduce the heat, add the tomato coulis and the tomato purée and stir in well. Bring the sauce to the boil and add the baccalà cut roughly into 2cm/1in squares. Reduce the heat and let the sauce gently simmer for 1 hour. Season with the anchovies and a generous sprinkling of black pepper.

•

Serve this sauce with either soft polenta (page 99) or tagliatelle. Sprinkle finely chopped parsley on top. Scraps of baccalà can be used for this dish.

BEAN AND SAUSAGE SAUCE
SALSA DI FAGIOLI E SALSICCE

SERVES 8

170g/5½oz dry borlotti beans

100g/3½oz sausage meat

150g/5oz Parma ham

100g/3½oz celery, finely chopped

100g/3½oz carrot, finely chopped

100g/3½oz onion, finely chopped

2 cloves garlic, finely chopped

1kg/2¼lb tomatoes, peeled, seeded and finely chopped

1 glass extra-virgin olive oil

Soak the beans overnight. Cook the beans in unsalted water; this will take about 1 hour depending on the age of the beans.

•

Fry the sausage meat and Parma ham in the olive oil, add the celery, carrot, onion and garlic, and fry until soft. Add the tomato and gently cook for half an hour.

•

Drain the beans and add to the tomato sauce. Cook the beans and tomato sauce together for 15 minutes. Some of the beans will break up and thicken the sauce.

•

Serve this sauce with tagliatelle and Parmesan cheese.

Black and White Tagliatelle with Smoked Salmon

TAGLIATELLE NERO E BIANCO CON SALMONE FUMIGATO

SERVES 6

Pasta

500g/1lb 2oz Farina O flour

2 tablespoons olive oil

4 eggs

a little tepid water

ink from 3 or 4 squid

pinch of salt

Sauce

2 shallots, finely chopped

2 tablespoons olive oil

40g/1½oz butter

200ml/7fl oz dry white wine

200ml/7fl oz single cream

¼ teaspoon dry dill

a little fresh lemon juice

125g/4½oz smoked salmon, cut into julienne

salt and freshly ground black pepper

a few sprigs dill

1 tablespoon chopped chive

Mix all pasta ingredients together except the ink. Divide the mixture in two, adding the ink to one lot only. Knead the dough and roll out in the usual way (page 72). Cut the sheets on the tagliatelle cutter of the pasta machine.

•

To make the sauce. Sweat the finely chopped shallots in oil and butter, add the wine and allow to almost evaporate, add the cream, ¼ teaspoon of dry dill, a few drops of lemon juice and bring to the boil. Reduce the heat to very low.

•

To serve. Cook the pasta in plenty of salted water. When al dente, strain and mix with sauce. Take the pan off the heat, add the smoked salmon and season.

•

Mix well, garnish the pasta with small sprigs of dill, sprinkle with chopped chive, and serve at once.

Tagliatelle with Lamb Sauce
TAGLIATELLE CON SUGO D'AGNELLO

SERVES 4

450g/1lb fresh tagliatelle (page 84)

600g/1lb 5oz lamb, finely chopped

olive oil

1 onion, finely chopped

2 cloves garlic, finely chopped

450g/1lb tomatoes, peeled and finely chopped

salt and freshly ground black pepper

2 fresh red chillies, seeded and finely chopped

pinch of dried chilli flakes

1 glass dry white wine

2 tablespoons finely chopped parsley

dry pecorino cheese for grating on top

Fry the lamb in olive oil until sealed. Remove and reserve. Add the onion and garlic to the pan and fry until golden and soft. Stir in the tomatoes and cook briefly.

•

Return the lamb to the tomato mixture. Season with salt, pepper and fresh chillies and dry chilli flakes. Add the white wine and a little water, and cook for 30 minutes. Add the parsley at the last moment and check the seasoning.

•

Serve *sugo d'agnello* on top of the tagliatelle, with pecorino cheese grated over.

•

This recipe comes from the mountainous region of the Abruzzi, just south of the Marche region, where lamb is plentiful. It is almost unknown in the other regions of Italy for lamb to be used in a sauce. In the Abruzzi area, the pasta served with this sauce would be maccheroni alla chitarra. *The noodles are cut on a 'guitar', a rectangular frame strung with a large number of wires.*

Deep-fried Stuffed Pasta Triangles
PANZAROTTI

These morsels are served as an appetizer with pre-dinner drinks. If you are short of time, wonton wrappers (obtainable from oriental supermarkets) can be used in place of the pasta dough. These also give a lighter and crisper result. Simply seal with beaten egg and press the edges together. Deep-fry in the same way.

●

To make the pasta. Sift the flour onto a pastry board and make a well in the centre. Add 2 pinches of salt, the oil and the egg yolks and about 2 tablespoons of warm water. Knead the mixture into a firm dough, adding a little more water if necessary. Knead the dough thoroughly until smooth and elastic, then put in a polythene bag and leave it to rest in a fridge for about half an hour.

●

For the filling. Mix the ricotta, mozzarella and Parmesan with the Parma ham, season to taste with salt, pepper and a pinch of freshly grated nutmeg.

●

To assemble the panzarotti. Roll out the dough on a floured board until 2mm/$\frac{1}{10}$in thick, and cut into 7.5cm/3in squares. Place a heaped teaspoon of filling in the centre of each square of pasta. Brush the edges of the pasta with the beaten egg and water mixture and fold corner-to-corner to make a triangle. Seal the edges lightly together using a fork.

●

SERVES 6

Pasta

600g/1¼lb plain flour

salt

150ml/¼pt olive oil

4 eggs yolks

Filling

175g/6oz fresh ricotta

175g/6oz mozzarella, diced small

6 tablespoons freshly grated Parmesan cheese

60g/2oz Parma ham or salami, minced

salt and freshly ground black pepper

freshly grated nutmeg

1 egg, beaten with 1 teaspoon water

grated Parmesan, for sprinkling

Deep-fry the triangles until puffed up, lightly golden and crisp. Drain well on absorbent kitchen paper and serve hot, sprinkled with Parmesan cheese.

PENNE WITH RICOTTA CHEESE AND SAUSAGE

PENNE ALLA PASTORA

SERVES 4

300g/10oz ridged penne

400g/14oz ricotta

150g/5oz Italian sausage

freshly ground black pepper

freshly grated pecorino cheese

2 tablespoons olive oil

Remove the skins from the sausages and break them up into small pieces. Gently cook the sausage meat in the olive oil, do not allow it to get over browned.

•

Meanwhile, boil the penne in abundant salted water.

•

Sieve the ricotta cheese into a serving bowl, add a little water from the pasta water and a lot of coarsely ground black pepper. Blend the cheese until it has the consistency of a creamy paste. Add the sausage meat, drained of the oil, to the ricotta, and fold in.

•

When the penne reach al dente, drain, but not too thoroughly. Stir the pasta into the ricotta and sausage mixture. Serve with grated pecorino cheese.

BIGOLI WITH CHICKEN LIVER SAUCE

BIGOLI COI ROVINASSI (SALSA DI FEGATINI DI POLLO)

To make the bigoli. Mix the ingredients and make a dough. Knead for 10 minutes. Pass through a spaghetti cutting machine, but failing this, pass through the tagliatelle blades on a pasta machine. In Italy a special cutting machine is used for making bigoli but adequate results are achieved using the above method. Leave the pasta to rest for 1 hour before boiling.

•

Boil the pasta in abundant boiling salted water until al dente.

•

Heat the olive oil and butter in a frying pan. When the butter is foaming, add the garlic and sage and sauté until the garlic is golden. Add the chicken livers, sauté briskly for 1 or 2 minutes. Pour the Marsala and wine over the livers and let them cook briskly until the wines become glazed. Season with salt and pepper to taste. Pour the chicken liver sauce over the bigoli, with freshly grated Parmesan sprinkled on top.

SERVES 4–6

Bigoli

250g/9oz wholewheat flour

90g/3oz plain flour

6 large eggs

salt

Liver sauce

350g/12oz chicken livers, cleaned and cut into small pieces

4 tablespoons extra-virgin olive oil

90g/3oz butter

2 cloves garlic, finely chopped

4 teaspoons finely chopped sage leaves

4 tablespoons Marsala

4 tablespoons dry white wine

salt and freshly ground black pepper

freshly grated Parmesan cheese

UKRAINIAN RAVIOLI WITH POTATO AND ONION
VARENIKI

SERVES 6

Filling

1 large onion

$1\frac{1}{2}$ tablespoons sunflower oil

2 cups mashed potato

good pinch of salt

good pinch of freshly ground black pepper

Sauce

350g/$\frac{3}{4}$lb bacon, cut into julienne

4 tablespoons sunflower oil

2 onions, finely chopped

Dough

3 eggs

1 teaspoon salt

$2\frac{1}{2}$ cups milk or water

700g/1lb 9oz plain flour

This recipe was one which came to us via three Ukrainian students who came to stay with us. Their recipes were always cheap, filling, but nevertheless delicious. The first time I took them to a supermarket one of them took to his bed with a severe headache, he was so overcome by all the food which could be purchased. We always had a joke when cooking with them: was the recipe pre-revolution or post-revolution? If they replied post-revolution, we always reminded them we could get all the ingredients here. This was especially true when we made pashka *(Easter cake) one Easter. They were very excited that they could make it like great-grandma used to make it.*

•

To make the filling. Chop the onion finely and fry in the sunflower oil until the onion looks slightly caramelized. Keep stirring the onions to obtain this result, then add the onion to the mashed potato, and season with salt and pepper.

•

To make the sauce. Fry the bacon in the sunflower oil and remove when cooked with a perforated spoon. Add the finely chopped onions and fry until a deep golden brown, return the bacon.

•

To make the dough. Beat the eggs, salt and milk together in a mixing bowl, then add the flour gradually and work in thoroughly with your hands until a fairly stiff dough is formed, adding more milk/water if necessary. Knead the dough on a lightly floured surface, then cover the dough with a cloth and leave to rest for 1 hour.

•

To prepare the vareniki. Roll out the dough to a thickness of 1mm/$\frac{1}{16}$in. Cut the sheet into 10cm/4in rounds. Place a teaspoon of filling on each round and fold into half-moons. Crimp the edges with a fork to seal them.

•

Place the vareniki on tea towels until ready to cook them. Bring a large pot of salted water to the boil, drop in the vareniki and boil for about 5 minutes or until they rise to the surface. Remove with a slotted spoon to a serving dish, pour the fried bacon, onion and oil on top and serve immediately.

•

If you have some vareniki left over, they are delicious reheated by pan-frying in a little sunflower oil until they are a light golden colour.

Buckwheat Tagliatelle with Wild Mushroom Sauce
PIZZOCCHERI CON SALSA DI FUNGHI SALVATICI

SERVES 4

Pasta

200g/7oz buckwheat flour

75g/3oz strong white flour

3 eggs

pinch of salt

Sauce

3 cloves garlic, finely chopped

2 tablespoons extra-virgin olive oil

1 tablespoon flatleaf parsley, finely chopped

450g/1lb mixed wild mushrooms, sliced

3 tablespoons fresh tomato purée

salt and freshly ground black pepper

freshly grated Parmesan cheese

First make the pizzoccheri. Mix the flours together, add the salt. Make a well in the centre of the flour. Break the eggs into the well and make a dough. Knead till firm. Cut the dough on the tagliatelle cutter of a pasta machine.

•

To make the sauce. Fry the chopped garlic in the olive oil until slightly golden. Add the parsley and mushrooms and fry briskly. Lower the heat, add the tomato purée and season to taste. Cook for 5 minutes.

•

Cook the pasta in plenty of salted boiling water until al dente. Serve the tagliatelle with the wild mushroom sauce on top, sprinkled with fresh Parmesan.

Risotto with Truffles
RISOTTO CON TARTUFI

Heat the stock.

•

Melt half the butter with the oil in a large heavy saucepan and sauté the onion gently until transparent and lightly gold in colour.

•

Add the rice and stir it in thoroughly, but gently, to absorb all the butter and oil. Stir for 5 minutes then add the glass of wine and cook until absorbed.

•

Add 1 cup of boiling stock and cook, stirring until absorbed, then add another cup of boiling stock, and continue the process until all the stock has been used up and absorbed by the rice. This takes about 20 minutes. Turn off the heat.

•

Add the remainder of the butter and the Parmesan cheese and gently but thoroughly stir in. Cover the pan and let the risotto settle for 2 minutes.

•

Serve with the white truffle shaved on top, and extra Parmesan to sprinkle.

SERVES 6

750g/1½lb risotto rice (Arborio)

15g/½oz truffle—more if you feel generous

½ onion, finely chopped

2 litres/4pt chicken stock

1 glass wine

90g/3oz butter

1 tablespoon olive oil

90g/3oz freshly grated Parmesan cheese

Risotto with Bresoala
RISOTTO CON BRESOALA

SERVES 6

400g/14oz risotto rice (Arborio)

115g/4oz bresoala, cut in wide strips

1 onion, finely chopped

60g/2oz butter

3 sage leaves

1 bay leaf

4 tomatoes, peeled, seeded and diced, about 200g/7oz

50ml/2fl oz dry white wine

1 litre/1¾pt meat stock

2 tablespoons finely chopped parsley

salt and freshly ground black pepper

100g/3½oz freshly grated Parmesan cheese

Finely chop the onion and gently fry it in a large heavy pan in a little of the butter until golden. Add the sage, bay leaf and diced tomatoes. If the tomatoes are not ripe, add ½ tablespoon tomato purée. Season with salt and pepper.

•

Add the rice, wine and stock. Bring the stock to the boil, reduce the heat and gently simmer, stirring occasionally. When the rice is cooked, add the parsley and the bresoala together with the rest of the butter. The end result should be of risotto consistency, creamy but with rice grains still firm to the bite.

•

Serve with freshly grated Parmesan cheese.

Basic Polenta

Bright sunshine-yellow polenta is made from ground maize meal. An instant polenta flour is available, it is not quite as good as the original method, but is not a bad substitute if you are pressed for time.

SERVES 4

900ml/1½pt boiling salted water

300g/10oz polenta flour

olive oil

•

Add the flour to the boiling water (the water must be boiling because a high temperature is needed to burst the starch grains), letting it drop in like sand sifting through your fingers. As the flour is falling into the water, stir with a wooden spoon. Always stir in one direction, never change direction. Keep stirring for 30–40 minutes. You should end up with quite a thick paste, but not so thick as not to pour onto a tray.

•

Pour the polenta onto a lightly oiled tin, 2.5cm/1in deep. Leave to get cold and cut into diamond or oblong shapes. Either grill on a griddle or shallow fry in olive oil until golden. Serve straight away.

POLENTA *Traditionally a large copper pan, a* paiolo, *was used to make polenta. The base of the pan was rounded to make the stirring of the polenta easier and it was hung over a wood fire. A heavy casserole is used nowadays or a copper pan with an electric stirrer attached to it.*

The people of the Marche region are known as magna pulentoni, *polenta eaters. Polenta was the basic diet until just after the Second World War. With prosperity, polenta got forgotten but now it is back in fashion, no longer the food of the peasant classes.*

Polenta is made in two basic ways, soft or firm. Soft polenta used to be poured onto a large wooden board called a spianatoia. *The family would unite twice a day to eat polenta, spooning it with a simple sauce directly from the board. The firm variety was left to get cold, cut with a strong cotton thread into slices, and either charcoal grilled or fried in olive oil. It was served with game or used instead of bruschetta with a variety of toppings.*

Polenta was practically a symbol of family unification. In the dialect of the Marche they used to say, "Lu poro contadi, fatiga e stenta, lu mejo pastu sua è la pulenta"—*the poor farmer, tired and weary, his best meal is polenta.*

Polenta replaces bread, pasta, potatoes and other basic starch foods.

POLENTA FRITTERS

FRITELLE DI POLENTA

SERVES 6

Fritters

350g/12oz polenta flour

1 litre/1¾pt milk, plus 1 ladle

300g/10oz Fontina cheese

To make the sauce. In a frying pan, heat the olive oil and add the onion, the scraps of Parma ham, thyme and bay leaf. Add the tomatoes, season with salt and freshly ground black pepper and a pinch of sugar.

•

Leave to cook for half an hour, stirring from time to time. Pass the mixture through a sieve and check seasoning.

To make the polenta. **Bring the milk to the boil with 8g/¼oz of salt, keeping 1 ladleful aside.**

●

Add the polenta flour to the milk a little at a time, stirring continuously with a wooden spoon in a clockwise movement. When the polenta flour starts to thicken add the rest of the milk. Stir the polenta for at least 45 minutes. Cooking polenta for a long time makes it more digestible and eliminates the rather bitter taste of the polenta flour.

●

When the polenta starts coming away from the sides of the pan, it is nearly ready, but continue stirring until it has a very thick consistency.

●

Tip the polenta onto a marble pastry slab and with a palette knife dipped into hot water, smooth out the polenta to a thickness of approximately 1cm/½in. A rolling pin can be used instead if preferred.

●

Cut the polenta into 8cm/3in circles with a pastry cutter. To assemble the fritters, keep rolling out the off-cuts until all the polenta is used up. Place a slice of Fontina cheese on half of the circles, then top with a piece of Parma ham. Place the other polenta circles on top and gently press them down.

●

Dip the polenta in the beaten egg and then in the breadcrumbs. Fry the polenta fritters in olive oil, then drain on absorbent kitchen paper. Serve hot with the tomato sauce.

24 slices Parma ham, cut in half

1 beaten egg

fresh breadcrumbs made from day-old bread or Japanese breadcrumbs

olive oil (sufficient for deep-frying)

Sauce

1½kg/3½lb plum tomatoes, roughly chopped

1 small onion, finely chopped

100g/3½oz finely chopped Parma ham (use scraps)

1 tablespoon olive oil

pinch of thyme

1 bay leaf

salt and freshly ground black pepper

pinch of sugar

FRIED POLENTA AND SAUSAGE GNOCCHI
SURICITTI DI MACERATA

SERVES 4

500g/1lb 2oz polenta flour

1½litres/2½pt water

400g/14oz sausage meat (plain or liver)

150g/5oz plain white flour

grated zest of 1 lemon

salt and freshly ground black pepper

oil for deep frying

Make the polenta from the polenta flour and water (page 99). Leave to get cold.

•

Cook the sausage meat in a little olive oil, drain and reserve. When the sausage and polenta are cold, combine them and then add the flour and lemon zest. Season with salt and pepper. Mix thoroughly together, make into large gnocchi by rolling into long sausages, then cutting in 5cm/2in lengths. Deep-fry until golden.

•

Excellent served as a nibble or with game.

•

These suricitti *were made during the month of December in the Maceratese countryside. The name means little mice, which they are supposed to resemble. I find it hard to see the resemblance!*

Polenta alla Marchigiana

SERVES 4–6

300g/10oz polenta flour

200g/7oz Parma ham, cut in small strips (or the same quantity of Italian sausage meat)

2 cloves garlic, finely chopped

100g/3½oz grated pecorino or Parmesan cheese

extra-virgin olive oil

salt and freshly ground black pepper

Bring 1 litre/1¾pt of salted water to the boil and, gently stirring, add the polenta flour, letting it trickle through your fingers like sand or falling rain. Lower the heat and continue stirring for 45 minutes.

•

In a little olive oil, fry the garlic and Parma ham briefly, and add to the polenta mixture.

•

Stir in the grated cheese, season with freshly ground black pepper and check if sufficiently salted.

•

Pour onto a marble slab and leave to go cold. Cut into oblongs, 9cm/3½in × 5cm/2in. Cook on a hot griddle till crisp on either side.

•

Serve with game.

BAKED POLENTA WITH RICOTTA
POLENTA CUMEDADA

SERVES 6

600g/1lb 5oz cooked, cold polenta (page 99)

600g/1lb 5oz fresh ricotta

300g/10oz finely chopped onion

60g/2oz butter

350ml/12fl oz milk

pinch of freshly grated nutmeg

freshly grated Parmesan cheese

salt and freshly ground black pepper

Gently fry the onion in the butter until golden, season with salt, freshly ground black pepper and a pinch of nutmeg. Add the milk and cook over a low flame for half an hour.

•

Lightly butter a gratin dish, put a layer of polenta thinly sliced, then some ricotta scattered on top and a little of the onion sauce, then a sprinkling of freshly grated Parmesan. Continue layering, finishing with the onion sauce and a lot of Parmesan. Place the polenta in a preheated oven set at 220°C/425°F/gas 7 and cook until the top is golden.

ETRUSCAN-STYLE CANNELLONI
CANNELLONI ETRUSCO

SERVES 4

Pasta

200g/7oz Farina O flour

1 egg, plus 1 egg yolk

salt

Make the pasta from the listed ingredients following the method for lasagnette (see page 110), but cutting the pasta into 10cm/4in squares. Boil the pasta in plenty of salted water until al dente, drain and leave on a dry linen cloth.

•

Béchamel sauce. Melt the butter in a saucepan, add the flour and gently cook over a low heat for 2–3 minutes, stirring constantly. Add the warmed milk and using a balloon whisk, stir for 5 minutes, season with salt. Make sure there are no lumps in the sauce. Reserve two-thirds of the sauce for later, one-third to mix with the filling.

•

Slice the mushrooms and cook in 2 tablespoons extra-virgin olive oil. Stir them into one-third of the béchamel sauce. Add 3 tablespoons of grated Parmesan, the julienne of Parma ham, and season with salt and freshly ground black pepper. Fold all the ingredients in well.

•

Place a generous spoonful of this mixture on each square of pasta and roll up. Place the cannelloni in a single layer on a well-buttered gratin dish. To the remaining two-thirds béchamel, add the cup of milk and reheat. Pour this béchamel on top of the cannelloni and sprinkle with grated Parmesan and gruyère cheeses. Bake in a hot oven set at 230°C/450°F/gas 8 for 15 minutes.

Béchamel

50g/1½oz butter

50g/1½oz flour

500ml/¾pt warmed milk

1 cup milk

salt

Filling

300g/10oz wild mushrooms, sliced (preferably mixed, but porcini on their own are fine)

2 tablespoons extra-virgin olive oil

3 tablespoons grated Parmesan

50g/1½oz Parma ham cut in julienne

salt and freshly ground black pepper

50g/1½oz grated gruyère

50g/1½oz grated Parmesan

1 cup milk

Cannelloni Rossini

SERVES 4

8 squares cannelloni pasta, 11cm/4½in square

90g/3oz veal

90g/3oz chicken breast

125g/4½oz chicken livers

20g/¾oz dried porcini mushrooms, soaked in warm water for half an hour, drained and dried

1 medium carrot

1 stick celery

1 medium onion

1 wine glass Marsala

50g/1½oz freshly grated Parmesan cheese

2 eggs

salt and freshly ground black pepper

pinch of nutmeg

3 tablespoons olive oil

4 tablespoons tomato coulis (page 107)

Béchamel

20g/¾oz butter

20g/¾oz flour

450ml/¾pt milk, warmed

salt and freshly ground white pepper

Make the pasta as described on page 110, but cutting the pasta into 11cm/4½in squares. Finely chop and fry in olive oil the carrot, onion and celery. Add the veal, chicken and livers, all roughly chopped. Fry over high heat to seal, pour in the Marsala, add the salt, pepper and porcini mushrooms roughly chopped. Cook gently until the Marsala has evaporated.

•

Put this mixture in a food processor and process finely. Stir in the Parmesan cheese, eggs and nutmeg.

•

To make the béchamel. Melt the butter in a small pan. Add the flour and stir in with a wooden spoon. Add the milk, salt and pepper, cook until thickened and smooth.

•

To assemble. Divide the mixture between the 8 squares of pasta and roll up into sausage shapes. Place on a buttered gratin dish, pour béchamel sauce on top and a little fresh tomato sauce and freshly grated Parmesan cheese. Bake in a hot oven 230°C/450°F/gas 8 for 15 minutes.

TOMATO COULIS
SALSA DI POMODORO

Roughly chop the tomatoes. Gently fry the onion and garlic in the olive oil until soft and golden, add the tomatoes and cook until soft. Season the sauce with salt and pepper. Pass the tomato mixture through a vegetable mill.

•

When making this sauce it is a good idea to make extra and keep it in the deep freeze for use at a later date.

•

Always remember that summer tomatoes are best for this sauce so make a batch before winter sets in. It is a sauce used so often in Italian cooking that it is possible to buy a machine in Italy for puréeing the tomatoes from fresh. It is called a passa pomodoro, *and is well worth buying if you should see one on a trip to Italy. The machine, which is not very expensive, also makes very good fruit drinks from peaches, pears, apricots etc.*

MAKES 900ML/1½PT

1kg/2¼lb very ripe tomatoes (preferably plum)

2 tablespoons finely chopped onion

2 tablespoons garlic, finely chopped

2 tablespoons extra-virgin olive oil

salt and freshly ground black pepper

PASSATELLI PESARO-STYLE
PASSATELLI PESARESI

SERVES 4–6

Sauce

2.8ml/5pt meat stock

1 cup barley

1 onion, finely chopped

2 large carrots, finely chopped

2 stalks celery, finely chopped

salt and freshly ground black pepper

Dough

400g/14oz very fine, fresh white breadcrumbs

200g/7oz freshly grated Parmesan cheese

5 eggs

salt and freshly ground black pepper

pinch of freshly grated nutmeg

pinch of ground cinnamon

finely grated zest of 1 lemon

Passatelli are only found in Emilia Romagna and the northern part of the Marche. A special tool is used for making passatelli, which consists of a perforated concave metal disc with two wooden handles. A potato ricer with large holes will do as a substitute. A mouli-légume with large holes can also be used for this operation. Passatelli can also be served as a soup, which is more common. Just cook the passatelli in the broth, ladle out and serve with grated Parmesan cheese.

•

Make the sauce first. Bring the stock to the boil and add the vegetables and barley when the latter are partially cooked. When the vegetables are cooked, season to taste. Blend all the ingredients together to a thick sauce.

•

To make the dough. Mix together the bread-crumbs, Parmesan, eggs, salt, pepper, nutmeg, cinnamon and lemon zest. All the ingredients must be mixed thoroughly, preferably by hand for about 10 minutes. The resulting mixture will be quite a solid dough. Leave the dough for at least 2 hours in a fridge, longer if possible.

•

Reheat the sauce and keep it warm over a low heat.

•

Deep-fry the artichoke slices which have been thoroughly dried. Drain them on absorbent paper, and sprinkle with salt.

•

Bring the meat broth or salted water to the boil. Squeeze the dough through a potato ricer with large holes, making cylinders 2.5cm/1in long, straight into the boiling broth. You need strong hands for this operation. When the passatelli rise to the surface, remove them with a perforated spoon. Put them onto a puddle of the sauce, sprinkle with deep-fried artichokes, slivers of Parmesan and julienne of sun-dried tomato. Serve at once.

2 litres/3½pt meat broth or salted water

20 small purple artichokes, finely sliced (keep in acidulated water)

oil for deep-frying

slivers of Parmesan cheese

30 halves of sun-dried tomato cut into julienne

Lasagnette with Ragout of Ceps

LASAGNETTE CON PORCINI IN UMIDO

SERVES 4

Pasta

300g/10oz Farina O flour

3 eggs

salt

Ceps

3 cloves garlic, finely chopped

3 tablespoons extra-virgin olive oil

handful of finely chopped mint

450g/1lb porcini, thinly sliced

½ cup light chicken stock

3 tablespoons fresh tomato coulis (page 107)

salt and freshly ground black pepper

freshly grated Parmesan cheese

Mix the flour with the eggs and salt to make a smooth dough. Roll the dough out thinly through a pasta machine, with the final setting at number ½, and cut into 7.5cm/3in squares.

•

Fry the chopped garlic in extra-virgin olive oil until golden, add the finely chopped mint and thinly sliced porcini and fry briskly. Lower the heat, add the stock and tomato coulis. Cook the porcini until tender and season with salt and pepper.

•

Cook the pasta in plenty of boiling salted water until al dente.

•

To serve. Place 2 squares of freshly cooked pasta on each plate, add the ragout of porcini and place 2 squares of pasta on top. Sprinkle with freshly grated Parmesan.

Seafood Lasagne
LASAGNE ALLA MARINARA

SERVES 6

Fish sauce

450g/1lb prawns, shells on

450g/1lb Dublin Bay prawns, shells on

225g/½lb scallops, cleaned

225g/½lb monkfish

225g/½lb small squid, cleaned

1 small lobster, weighing about 450g/1lb

1 onion, finely chopped

1 carrot, finely chopped

2 cloves garlic, finely chopped

2 stalks celery, finely chopped

450g/1lb tomatoes, chopped

1 litre/1¾pt water

extra-virgin olive oil

bouquet garni of thyme, parsley, celery tops and bay leaf

2 knobs butter

¼ cup flour

1 tablespoon tomato purée

salt and freshly ground black pepper

generous pinch of dried chilli flakes

freshly grated Parmesan cheese

Béchamel

1.2 litres/2½pt hot milk

60g/2oz flour

60g/2oz butter

salt and pepper to taste

Pasta

750g/1½lb flour

2 egg yolks

4 whole eggs

pinch of salt

Make wide sheets of pasta as on page 72. The final setting on the pasta machine should be number 1.

•

Dice the monkfish into 1cm/½in squares, fry gently in a little olive oil, and reserve.

•

Slice the scallops in 3 across the grain and fry them in olive oil. Reserve.

•

Boil the squid for 10 minutes. Slice the squid into thinnish rings and reserve.

•

If prawns and Dublin Bay prawns are uncooked, first boil them in salted water for 5 minutes. If the lobster is live, boil that in salted water for 5 minutes too.

•

Shell all shellfish and reserve the shells. Fry in olive oil the onion, carrot, garlic and celery. Add the shells and fry for 2–3 minutes. Add the tomatoes and fry until soft. Add 1 litre/1¾pt water and bouquet garni, and simmer for 1 hour. Strain the mixture through a chinois, return the sauce to the heat, add a beurre manié made from the butter worked with the flour, blend in well and cook for 10 minutes. Add the tomato purée, season with salt, pepper and chilli pepper flakes. Leave the sauce to cool. Add fish to the tomato sauce.

•

To make the béchamel. Melt the butter and add the flour. Stir in well, add the milk and beat in until the sauce is smooth. Cook, stirring all the time, for 5 minutes. Season with salt and freshly ground black pepper.

•

To assemble the lasagne. Butter a lasagne dish, put a layer of fish sauce, a thin layer of béchamel and a little Parmesan cheese scattered over. Cover with a layer of pasta. Continue layering until all the sauce and pasta are used up, finish with a layer of béchamel, sprinkled with Parmesan. Bake in a hot oven, 230°C/450°F/gas 8, for 20 minutes.

Lasagne Bolognese

SERVES 4

Pasta

450g/1lb Farina O flour, or strong plain flour

3 eggs

175g/6oz cooked spinach, well drained and puréed

salt

Béchamel

50g/1½oz butter

2 tablespoons flour

750ml/1¼pt milk

salt and pepper

pinch of nutmeg

90g/3oz freshly grated Parmesan cheese

Ragù bolognese

350g/12oz lean minced beef

90g/3oz streaky bacon

olive oil

1 onion finely chopped

1 carrot finely chopped

2 stalks celery, finely chopped

150ml/¼pt dry white wine

300ml/½pt water

3 tablespoons tomato purée

2 sprigs parsley, chopped

1 bay leaf

salt and pepper

To make the pasta. Pour the flour into a mixing bowl and make a well in the centre. Lightly beat the eggs and then mix into the flour with the spinach and salt. Work lightly into a rough ball and knead on a floured board for a few minutes until the dough is smooth, shiny and elastic. Wrap in greaseproof paper and leave for 30 minutes to rest. If making by hand, divide the dough into four balls and flatten out each one, rolling lengthways. Keep the surface well floured. Continue until the pasta is paper-thin, then cut into wide strips. If using a hand pasta machine the final thickness should be number 1 setting.

•

Have ready a large pan of boiling water. Place the lasagne in the boiling water and when it rises to the top (this should take about 2 minutes), drain and dip straight away into a bowl of cold water, then drain again and leave out flat on clean linen cloths.

•

To make the ragù. First mince the bacon and fry in a little olive oil. Add the onion, carrot, celery and when they have slightly browned, add the beef and seal it.

•

Add the wine, water and tomato purée, parsley, bay leaf and seasoning. Cover the pan and simmer for 30–40 minutes.

•

For the béchamel sauce. Melt the butter in a saucepan, then add the flour and stir well. Add the milk, which has been heated but not boiled, a little at a time, stirring all the time. Season with salt, pepper and nutmeg. Cook for 15 minutes, stirring occasionally to ensure a creamy sauce. Use a balloon whisk for this process.

•

To assemble the lasagne. Take a rectangular gratin dish (earthenware or stainless steel) approximately 30×20×7.5cm/12×8×3in and spread a layer of ragù in the bottom and then a layer of béchamel sauce. Sprinkle with Parmesan and cover with pasta. Keep on layering in this way until the dish is full, finishing with a layer of béchamel, topped with a generous coating of Parmesan cheese.

•

Place the dish in a hot oven 190°C/375°F/gas 5 for about 30 minutes. Remove from the oven and leave to rest for a few minutes before serving. Serve with extra Parmesan cheese.

VINCISGRASSI

AN 18TH-CENTURY PASTA DISH

Vincisgrassi is a speciality of the Marche region of Italy, in particular of Macerata. The story goes that it was named after an Austrian general Windisch Graetz, who was with his troops in Ancona in 1799 during the Napoleonic war. Actually Antonio Nebbia, who wrote a gastronomic manual in 1784, mentioned in his book a similar dish called Princisgras.

•

Make a dough from the pasta ingredients, knead well and roll through a pasta machine as you would for lasagne. Cut the pasta lengths into squares approximately 12.5cm/5in square. Cook the squares in plenty of boiling salted water a few at a time. Place on linen cloths to drain.

•

For the sauce. Melt 50g/2oz of the butter, add the flour and blend in well. Add the milk, which has been previously heated, a little at a time beating well with a balloon whisk. Cook the porcini in the olive oil and add to the béchamel. Stir in the Parma ham. Add the cream and parsley, season, and bring to the boil. Turn off the heat.

•

To assemble the vincisgrassi. Butter a gratin dish and cover the bottom with a layer of pasta, then spread over a layer of béchamel, dot with butter and sprinkle with some Parmesan cheese. Continue the process making layer after layer, finishing with a béchamel layer and a sprinkling of Parmesan cheese. Cook in an oven preheated to 220°C/425°F/gas 7 for 20 minutes. Serve with a

SERVES 6

Pasta

500g/1lb2oz Farina O or strong plain flour

2 whole eggs, plus 4 egg yolks

1 teaspoon salt

Sauce

400g/14oz porcini, sliced

200g/7oz Parma ham, cut in julienne

1.2 litres/2pt milk

60g/2oz flour

150g/5oz butter

200g/7oz single cream

60ml/2fl oz extra-virgin olive oil

3 tablespoons finely chopped parsley

salt and freshly ground black pepper

(continued overleaf)

150g/5oz freshly grated Parmesan cheese

truffle oil, or if possible a little shaved white truffle

little truffle oil splashed on top or, better still, with shavings of white truffle, and a little Parmesan cheese.

VINCISGRASSI WITH MEAT
VINCISGRASSI CON CARNE

SERVES 4–6

For the pasta

500g/1lb 2oz Farina O or strong plain flour

2 whole eggs, plus 4 egg yolks

1 teaspoon salt

Meat sauce

115g/¼lb streaky bacon, minced

olive oil

2 cloves garlic

1 onion, finely chopped

1 stalk celery, finely chopped

1 carrot, finely chopped

The pasta can be made before or during the cooking of the sauce. Make a dough from the above ingredients and roll through the pasta machine as you would for lasagne (page 113). Cut the dough into squares approximately 12.5cm/5in square. Cook the squares in boiling water a few at a time, place on linen cloths to drain.

•

To make the meat sauce. Fry the bacon in olive oil. Add the chopped vegetables, fry until the onion is lightly golden. Add the minced meat and seal. Pour in the glass of wine and allow to bubble away. Add hot water, enough to cover the meat. Add the tomato purée, bay leaf and cloves. Season. Reduce the flame and simmer for about 2 hours, depending on the type of meat used. Add the finely chopped chicken livers and cook briefly. Check the seasoning.

•

To assemble the vincisgrassi. Lightly oil a gratin dish and put a layer of pasta, Parmesan and the meat sauce. Repeat this layering until the ingredients are used up, finishing with pasta. Sprinkle with Parmesan and dot with small knobs of butter.

•

Put the pasta in a moderate oven 190°C/375°F/ gas 5. As soon as the surface is browned, the pasta is ready. Serve with extra Parmesan.

450g/1lb lean minced beef

1 glass dry white wine

1 cup tomato purée

1 bay leaf

4 cloves

salt and freshly ground black pepper

175g/6oz finely chopped chicken livers

freshly grated Parmesan cheese

butter

Small Chestnut Gnocchi
GNOCCHETTI DI CASTAGNE

Pass the chestnuts and potato through the mouli-légume whilst still warm. Add the flour, egg yolk and salt to the chestnut and potato mixture. Knead all the ingredients together. Continue as for potato gnocchi (page 119).

•

Boil the gnocchi in plenty of salted water. When they rise to the top of the water, drain them. Toss the gnocchi in melted butter and sprinkle with Parmesan. Serve with pheasant or any other game cooked with a sauce.

SERVES 4

200g/7oz chestnuts, boiled and peeled

100g/3½oz boiled floury potato

70g/2½oz plain flour

1 egg yolk

salt

freshly grated Parmesan cheese

Spinach Gnocchi
GNOCCHI VERDI

SERVES 4

600g/1lb 5oz spinach, washed

250g/9oz ricotta, sieved

2 eggs

150g/5oz freshly grated Parmesan cheese

100g/3½oz butter

freshly grated nutmeg

3 tablespoons flour (if necessary)

salt

8 tablespoons tomato sauce (page 107)

Cook the spinach with a little salt—water is not necessary—and strain and squeeze it dry with your hands. Chop the spinach finely, add to a pan with melted butter and mix in well. Leave the spinach to cool. When cooled add the sieved ricotta and 100g/4oz of grated Parmesan, the eggs and a pinch of nutmeg. If the mixture is too soft, add 1 tablespoon of flour. Lightly flour a cloth, make the gnocchi by forming them into balls the size of a large marble, and dent the centre slightly with a thumb. Keep the hands lightly floured. As the gnocchi are prepared, leave them on the floured cloth.

•

Bring a large saucepan of lightly salted water to the boil. Boil the gnocchi for a few minutes, until they rise to the surface of the water.

•

Butter a gratin dish or 4 single ones, make one layer of the gnocchi and cover with tomato sauce. Sprinkle with the rest of the grated Parmesan cheese and pass under the grill until the cheese is coloured.

•

These gnocchi can also be served with melted butter infused with sage leaves.

Potato Gnocchi
GNOCCHI DI PATATE

SERVES 4

1kg/2¼lb floury potatoes, mashed

1 whole egg

250g/9oz plain flour

generous pinch of nutmeg

salt and freshly ground pepper

Boil the potatoes in their skins in salted water and peel them whilst they are still warm. Pass them immediately through a vegetable mill (mouli-légume). You should have 1kg/2¼lb mashed potato.

•

Add the egg, flour, and salt and pepper and work in well. Take pieces of the potato mixture and roll into thumb-thick rolls, then cut into short pieces 2–3cm/1in long. Now with the tip of the index finger, roll each cylinder over the inside curve of a long pronged fork. While pressing the potato cylinders with your finger, flip it away towards the handle, and let it drop onto a lightly floured tray. Do not be put off—it is not as complicated as it sounds. This "rolling" keeps the gnocchi light.

•

Boil the gnocchi in plenty of salted boiling water and as soon as they rise to the surface, remove them with a perforated spoon.

•

Serve gnocchi with tomato sauce (page 107), with shredded basil added to taste and freshly grated Parmesan cheese.

•

The potatoes can be cooked in their skins in a plain or convection microwave; it is really better than the boiling method.

MEAT

Meat and game feature more strongly on our menu during the autumn and winter months. Lamb is the exception: we have Welsh lamb all the year round and here in Wales we have what we consider the best lamb to be had. The early spring brings lowland lamb, summer the upland lamb and towards late summer through to late autumn the mountain lamb. The mountain lambs feed off pure grass and sweet herbs, and are born out of doors. We can also get salt marsh lamb which comes from around Cardigan Bay and the Gower peninsular.

We try to use as much organic meat as possible. Our pigs for porchetta come from a farm across the road from us and the rest of our meat comes from local farmer/butchers. Goats generally come from a farm the other side of the mountain behind us.

When the game season starts with grouse on 12 August, it always brings a sense of excitement. This must be because one never knows what is going to arrive from the shoots. Game is plentiful round here; the only type we have to bring in from Scotland is grouse because our local supply is limited. Pheasants are so abundant one can see them in almost every field.

We also have supplies of teal, woodcock, partridge, hare and rabbit. Venison is culled from woods not far from The Walnut Tree.

Domestic birds, such as turkeys, either bronze or Norfolk blacks, chickens and ducks, are also bred organically near us. Through living in the country our chefs learn to respect the meat they handle. They have seen the animals in the fields around us, heard the farmers talking about nights spent out in the sheep sheds or fields in the freezing cold, bringing lambs into the world. We encourage our chefs to go to the farms so that they can develop more feeling and understanding for the product. The chefs have to realize that meat does not just come portion-controlled, covered with a plastic wrap.

TOURNEDOS ROSSINI

SERVES 4

4 fillet steaks, weighing 200g/7oz each

4 croûtons (same size as the base of the steak)

90g/3oz pâté de foie gras in thin slices

1 black truffle, peel and cut 4 slices, chop the rest

2 tablespoons butter

1 tablespoon olive oil

100ml/3½fl oz Madeira or Marsala

200ml/7fl oz stock

salt and freshly ground black pepper

Heat the olive oil and butter in a frying pan, when foaming add the steaks. Cook over a strong heat, until medium or rare, as preferred. Season with salt and freshly ground black pepper. Remove from the pan and keep warm.

•

Drain the butter and oil from the pan and deglaze with the Madeira or Marsala, add the stock and reduce by one-third, skimming off any impurities. Strain the sauce and add the chopped truffle.

•

While the sauce is reducing, fry the 4 croûtons in butter. Put on each a slice of pâté de foie gras the same size as the croûton. Place under a hot grill for 2 minutes.

•

Place the steaks on top of the croûtons, a slice of truffle on top and pour the sauce over steaks.

Gioacchino Rossini, the composer gourmet, equally well known as a prolific opera composer and lover of good food, came from Pesaro in the Marche. He was born in 1792 and died in 1868. The best known dish named after him is Tournedos Rossini. Rossini is said to have given the recipe to the chef at the Café Anglais in Paris. In Rossini's own words, "To eat, to love, to sing, and to digest; in truth these are the four acts in this opera bouffe that we call life, and which vanishes like the bubbles in a bottle of champagne."

Tournedos Rossini was on our very first menu at The Walnut Tree.

STEAK MIRABEAU

SERVES 4

4 sirloin steaks

20 anchovy fillets

18 pitted black olives, halved

1 tablespoon olive oil

2 tablespoons butter

freshly ground black pepper

1 glass red wine

Heat the oil and butter in a frying pan and when it is foaming add the steaks. Cook as preferred and season with freshly ground black pepper. Criss-cross the steaks with 4 anchovy fillets and place the olive halves in the squares. Remove the steaks from the pan and keep warm. Mash the remaining 4 anchovy fillets in the pan juices, add a glass of red wine and reduce rapidly until a glaze appears on the sauce. Pour the sauce over the steaks and serve at once.

Steak with Five Peppers and Sultanas
BISTECCA AI CINQUE TIPI DI PEPE E UVA SULTANINA

SERVES 4

4 fillet steaks, weighing 175g/6oz each

10 fresh green peppercorns, crushed

2 pinches coarsely ground white pepper

2 pinches coarsely ground black pepper

2 pinches coarsely ground Schezuan pepper

2 small fresh red chilli peppers, seeded and finely sliced

1 tablespoon olive oil

1 knob of butter

4 tablespoons sultanas, soaked in 1 wine glass Marsala

1 cup strong meat stock

salt

Mix all the peppers together, divide into four and press into one side of the steaks.

•

Heat the oil and butter in a frying pan and when hot add the steaks. Cook, turning the steaks only when they are well sealed. Season with salt. Remove the steaks from the pan when they are cooked to your taste and keep warm.

•

Deglaze the frying pan with the Marsala drained from the sultanas and add 1 cup of strong meat stock. Reduce the sauce to a syrupy consistency, and skim whilst it is reducing. Strain the sauce and add the sultanas, reheat. Pour the sauce over the steaks.

Steak Rolls with Tomato Sauce
BRACIOLINE CON SALSA DI POMODORO

SERVES 4

12 slices chuck steak, weighing 90g/3oz each

12 slices streaky bacon

a bunch of parsley, finely chopped

2 tablespoons dried oregano

3 cloves garlic, finely chopped

60g/2oz pine kernels

100g/3½oz freshly grated Parmesan cheese

salt and fresh coarsely ground black pepper

olive oil

1.2kg/2½lb plum tomatoes, peeled and finely chopped

2 glasses dry white wine

4 tablespoons tomato purée

bouquet garni (celery, bay leaf and parsley)

Pound the slices of beef between 2 sheets of greaseproof paper. Put a slice of bacon on each piece of meat. Sprinkle over the parsley, oregano and garlic, and divide the pine kernels and Parmesan cheese between the pieces of meat. Season with salt and pepper, then roll up the pieces of steak and secure with a cocktail stick.

•

Heat some olive oil in a heavy casserole and fry the rolls until brown all over. Add the tomatoes and white wine and reduce the heat.

•

Dilute the tomato purée with a little hot water and add it to the casserole. Make sure meat rolls are covered with sauce. Season lightly and add the bouquet garni.

•

Cook for 2 hours. During the cooking, make sure that the sauce does not burn on the bottom by stirring frequently and adding, if necessary, a little boiling water. Do not allow the sauce to bubble fiercely or the meat will toughen; a gentle ripple must be maintained.

•

Check the meat after 2 hours; it may need longer cooking. Check the seasoning. Remove the cocktail sticks.

•

Traditionally, the rolls are served atop tagliatelle, which has been flavoured with the sauce.

Fillet Steak Cacciatora
BISTECCA ALLA CACCIATORA

Heat the oil in a frying pan, add the steak, cook until done to your taste, then season with salt and pepper. Remove from the pan and keep warm.

•

Add the chopped garlic to the pan and fry briefly, stir the red wine and Marsala into the pan juices, scraping the bottom of the pan with a wooden spoon. Reduce the wine until it has become a thick syrup. Add the fennel and tomato purée. Stir well into the wine and cook for 1 minute more.

•

Pour the sauce over the steak and decorate with chopped parsley.

SERVES 4

4 fillet steaks, weighing 175g/6oz each

2 tablespoons olive oil

salt and freshly ground black pepper

2 cloves garlic, finely chopped

300ml/½pt red wine

300ml/½pt Marsala

1 teaspoon fennel seeds, freshly ground

4 tablespoons tomato purée

chopped parsley for garnish

STEAK FLORENTINE
BISTECCA ALLA FIORENTINA

SERVES 4

4 T-bone steaks

8 tablespoons extra-virgin olive oil

4 cloves garlic, crushed

juice of ½ lemon

fresh sprigs of rosemary

freshly ground black pepper

salt

lemon wedges

Rub the steak with the oil, garlic, lemon juice, rosemary and pepper on both sides. Leave the steaks to marinate for 1 hour.

•

The steak is best cooked over a charcoal fire but a very hot grill can be substituted. Grill the steaks for 3–5 minutes on each side. Sprinkle with salt before serving and serve with lemon wedges.

GALETTES OF STRAW POTATOES

SERVES 4

4 large potatoes

salt and pepper

olive oil

Grate the potatoes on a large cheese grater and season with salt and pepper.

•

Heat a little olive oil in a non-stick frying pan. For each galette, place a large spoonful of grated potato in the pan and flatten out with a spatula so that a lacey effect is created. Fry until crisp on one side, then turn over and fry the other side. Dry the galettes on absorbent kitchen paper. Keep warm.

•

To serve with the medaglioni opposite.

Tournedos of Beef with Wild Mushrooms and Vin Santo

MEDAGLIONI DI MANZO CON FUNGHI DI BOSCO AL VIN SANTO

Before cooking the tournedos, make the potato galettes as described opposite. Fry the mushrooms lightly in a little olive oil, add the Parma ham and cook briefly. Reserve.

•

Fry the medaglioni in 2 tablespoons of olive oil (to medium-rare is preferable). Remove the steaks from the pan and leave to rest for a few minutes.

•

Deglaze the pan with Vin Santo and meat stock, add the thyme and season. Reduce the sauce until it has thickened.

•

To serve the medaglioni, place a galette of potatoes on the plate and top with a medaglione. Return the mushrooms and prosciutto to the sauce in the pan and heat briefly. Spoon some of the mushrooms and sauce around the medaglione and decorate with a slice of truffle on top of the steak.

SERVES 4

4 medaglioni (tournedos), weighing 175g/6oz each

225g/8oz wild mushrooms such as chanterelles

60g/2oz Parma ham, cut into julienne

½ glass Vin Santo, or sweet sherry

½ cup meat stock

fresh thyme, finely chopped

salt and freshly ground black pepper

olive oil

black truffles (optional)

Carré of Welsh Lamb with Wild Mushrooms

CARRÉ D'AGNELLO CON FUNGHI SELVATICI

SERVES 4

4 carrés or best ends of young Welsh lamb, each with 6 bones

Sauce

1 large onion, roughly chopped

2 medium carrots, chopped

3 sticks celery, chopped

2 bay leaves

125ml/4fl oz Marsala

1 tablespoon tomato purée

6 cloves garlic, crushed

sprig of rosemary

2 tablespoons olive oil

115g/4oz fresh breadcrumbs

1 teaspoon each of fresh chopped thyme, parsley and marjoram

Trim the lamb removing all the fat and clean the bones up to the eye of the meat. Set aside in a cold place while you prepare the sauce. Brown the trimmings from the lamb in a roasting tin, pour off all the surplus fat and transfer the remainder to a saucepan. Add the onion, carrots, celery and bay leaves to the roasting tin and brown well over a high heat or in the oven.

•

Add the Marsala to the tin and bring to the boil, scraping to incorporate all the cooking juices. Stir in the tomato purée and 850ml/1½pt of water and then transfer the contents of the roasting tin to the saucepan. Add the garlic and rosemary, bring to the boil, lower the heat and simmer for 1½ hours, skimming constantly. Push the contents of the pan through a fine sieve, then reduce to the consistency of single cream. Keep the sauce warm until needed.

•

Heat 2 tablespoons of olive oil in a frying pan and seal the lamb all over. Remove from the pan.

•

Mix the breadcrumbs with the chopped herbs and season with salt and pepper.

•

Brush the outer surface of the lamb with the beaten egg, then press a layer of breadcrumbs over the meat to make a crust. Roast the lamb in an oven 190°C/375°F/gas 5 for about 7 minutes or until the meat is cooked but still pink. Remove the meat from the oven and allow it to rest for 4 minutes.

•

Fry the mushrooms in 2 tablespoons of extra-virgin olive oil and season to taste.

•

Carve the lamb into double chops removing one bone. Serve with the sauce, wild mushrooms and grilled polenta (page 99). Leeks and Parma ham (page 221) are also good with this recipe.

•

During the mushroom season, a mushroom-picking fever descends on The Walnut Tree. As collecting becomes an absolute obsession, so the menu features more and more recipes using a variety of species.

salt and freshly ground black pepper

2 eggs, beaten

225g/8oz mixed wild mushrooms, such as ceps, chanterelles, oyster mushrooms, pieds de mouton, trompettes de mort

extra-virgin olive oil

Lamb with Polenta and Artichokes

AGNELLO CON POLENTA E CARCIOFO

SERVES 4

2 best ends of lamb (about 6 chops each)

olive oil

2 eggs, beaten for egg wash

Herb and breadcrumb coating

115g/4oz fresh breadcrumbs

1 teaspoon each of fresh thyme, parsley, chives, and oregano, finely chopped

salt and freshly ground black pepper

Sauce

600ml/1pt rich lamb stock flavoured with rosemary (page 130, omitting the tomato purée)

Reduce the stock by two-thirds, and keep warm.

•

Trim the lamb, removing all the fat, and clean the bones to the eye of the meat. Seal the lamb in a little olive oil.

•

To prepare the coating, mix the breadcrumbs, herbs and salt and pepper together. Brush the outer surface of the lamb with the beaten egg and then cover with the breadcrumb mixture, pressing well to bind the crumbs.

•

Place the lamb in a roasting tray and cook in an oven set at 190°C/375°F/gas 5 for about 7 minutes or until the meat is pink. Remove the meat from the oven and leave it to rest for 4 minutes.

•

Carve the meat into chops, pour the strained sauce on plates and place 3 chops on each plate. Serve with grilled *polenta alla marchigiana* (page 103) and fried artichokes (page 218).

WELSH LAMB WITH GARLIC SAUCE

SERVES 6

6 best end of Welsh lamb (each strip with 4–5 chops)

olive oil

2 eggs, beaten for egg wash

<u>*Herb and breadcrumb coating*</u>

115g/4oz fresh breadcrumbs

1 teaspoon each of chopped fresh chervil, tarragon, thyme, parsley, chives and basil

salt and freshly ground black pepper

<u>*Garlic sauce*</u>

3 heads of garlic (do not remove skins)

300ml/½pt white wine

300ml/½pt water

300ml/½pt lamb stock

salt and freshly ground black pepper

30 cloves garlic, peeled

olive oil

sprigs of thyme or mint

Trim the lamb, removing all the fat, and clean the bones up to the eye of the meat.

•

Prepare the garlic for the garnish. Bring the 30 peeled cloves of garlic to the boil in just enough water to cover them. Strain. Repeat this process 3 times, then leave to cool.

•

Deep-fry the garlic cloves in olive oil until golden and crisp on the outside, still soft on the inside. Drain and leave on kitchen paper.

•

Now make the sauce. Leaving the skins on the garlic, gently bring the heads to the boil in the mixture of white wine, water and lamb stock. Cook until tender. Pass the garlic mixture through a sieve, pressing well, then liquidize. Adjust the seasoning and consistency. It should be a pouring consistency. You may need to add more water. Keep warm.

•

Seal the lamb in oil.

•

To prepare the coating. Mix together the bread-crumbs, herbs and seasoning. Brush the outer surface of the lamb with the beaten egg, then cover with the breadcrumb mixture, pressing well to bind the crumbs. Place the lamb in a roasting tray and cook in an oven preheated to 220°C/425°F/ gas 7 for about 7 minutes, or until the meat is pink. Remove from the oven and leave to rest for 4 minutes.

•

Carve the meat into chops. Pour the garlic sauce onto the plates and arrange the chops on top. Garnish each plate with 5 cloves of the fried garlic and a sprig of thyme or mint.

FRIED LAMB CUTLETS

COSTOLETTINE D' AGNELLO FRITTE

SERVES 4

12 best end chops, all fat removed

4 egg yolks beaten with salt and freshly ground black pepper

flour

4 egg whites, lightly beaten

dry breadcrumbs

lemon wedges

extra-virgin olive oil

Gently beat the meat on the chops until it is flattened to almost double its size. Dip the chops in the beaten egg yolks, then dip them lightly in flour and then into the egg whites, and finally into the breadcrumbs. Fry the chops in a little olive oil and drain on absorbent kitchen paper. Serve them very hot with lemon wedges.

•

In the Marche region a fritto misto ascolano *consists of these lamb cutlets,* olive ascolane, crema fritta, *and fried artichokes.*

Kid with Orange, Marsala and Coriander
CAPRETTO CON SALSA DI ARANCIO, MARSALA E CORIANDOLO

We always have kid on the menu in the spring. So many people nearby have goats either for their milk or for their wool. If they have too many billies we have them. If you want to try this recipe, Halal butchers and some Italian shops sell kid meat and the butcher will chop it up for you. Kid meat is a sweet tender meat with hardly any fat. The recipe is adapted from a recipe from Elizabeth David's Italian Food.

SERVES 6

1.4–1.8kg/3–4lb kid meat on the bone, cut into portions

1 large onion

3 cloves garlic

2 tablespoons oregano

5 tomatoes, peeled, seeded and chopped

3 carrots, finely sliced

1 stick celery, finely sliced

4 strips orange zest

2 tablespoons crushed coriander seeds

1 wine glass dry white wine

1 wine glass Marsala wine

4 tablespoons extra-virgin olive oil

juice of 1 orange

fresh coriander leaves

salt and freshly ground black pepper

Get your butcher to chop the kid meat into portions.

●

Crush the garlic and rub it into the meat with the oregano. Slice the onion and fry it until golden in 2 tablespoons of extra-virgin olive oil, remove the onion from the oil and reserve.

●

Add 2 more tablespoons of extra-virgin olive oil to the frying pan and fry the pieces of meat until golden all over. Return the onions to the pan and add the peeled seeded and chopped tomatoes. When the tomatoes are soft add the carrots and celery, crushed coriander seeds, white wine and Marsala. Season with salt and freshly ground black pepper. Cover the pan and simmer for 2 hours.

●

Remove the meat from the sauce and keep warm. Sieve the sauce and add the juice of 1 orange. Briskly reduce the sauce until a glaze appears, pour over the meat pieces and garnish with fresh coriander leaves.

Mixed Boiled Meats
BOLLITO MISTO EMILIANO

SERVES 10–12

750g/1½lb beef brisket

500g/1lb 2oz veal silverside

1 capon

6 pieces marrow bone, about 7.5cm/3in each

1 cotechino (page 171)

1 bouquet garni

1 large onion studded with 5 cloves

4 sticks celery

1 leek, washed thoroughly

6 carrots

12 black peppercorns

2 teaspoons coarse sea salt

Stuffing

100g/3½oz Parma ham, minced

giblets and liver of the capon, cooked in a little butter and chopped finely

2 tablespoons finely chopped onion

Bring 6 litres/9pt of water to the boil in a large saucepan. Season with salt and peppercorns. Lower the heat to a simmer and put in the bouquet garni, all the vegetables, and the beef. It will take approximately 2½ hours to cook. After 45 minutes, add the veal and the capon. Cook the cotechino separately, punctured with a fork and wrapped in muslin, for 2 hours. 45 minutes before the beef is ready, add the marrow bones wrapped in muslin. Check during cooking, the times are only approximate for the beef, veal and capon; more or less time may be needed.

•

The capon can also be deboned and stuffed. Mix all the ingredients for the stuffing thoroughly. Stuff the deboned capon with the mixture and sew the bird up with strong white thread. Wrap in muslin. Add to the bollito with the veal as before.

•

Carve the bollito at table and serve with any of the following:

•

Crostini fried in olive oil, spread with English mustard and topped with bone marrow
Mostarda di Cremona
Mostarda di Venezia (Venezia mustard)
Salsa verde (green sauce)
Salsa di rafano (horseradish sauce)
Salsa di pomodoro e prosciutto di Parma (cooked tomato and Parma ham sauce)
Salsa rustica (raw tomato sauce)

•

Put a choice of 3 or 4 of these condiments on the table.

•

Bollito misto is a northern Italian dish that evolved because people liked to eat large quantities of meat but lacked an oven for roasting. The dish varies slightly from region to region.

1 clove garlic, finely chopped and cooked in a little butter

100g/3½oz fresh breadcrumbs, soaked in milk and squeezed dry

1 tablespoon finely chopped parsley

2 eggs

freshly ground black pepper

Salsa Verde

Process all the ingredients, except the pepper. Add extra-virgin olive oil a little at a time to make a semi-fluid sauce and finish with a tablespoon of vinegar. Add a generous amount of pepper.

•

To serve with bollito misto.

1 bunch parsley, finely chopped

3 fillets anchovies

2 pickled gherkins

1 boiled potato

1 clove garlic

pinch of salt

freshly ground black pepper

1 tablespoon vinegar

Cooked Tomato and Parma Ham Sauce
SALSA DI POMODORO E PROSCIUTTO DI PARMA

1.7kg/3¾lb tomatoes, peeled, seeded and chopped

1 tablespoon finely chopped onion

100g/3½oz Parma ham, finely minced

pinch of thyme

1 bay leaf

1 tablespoon flour

salt and freshly ground black pepper

pinch of sugar

2 tablespoons olive oil

Fry the onion in the olive oil, add the Parma ham, thyme and bay leaf. Remove the pan from the heat and stir in 1 tablespoon of flour, return the pan to the heat and cook gently for 3 minutes. Add the tomatoes, season with salt, pepper and sugar and cook for 45 minutes, stirring from time to time.

•

To serve with bollito misto.

SALSA RUSTICA

SERVES 4

5 tomatoes, peeled, seeded and chopped

2 cloves garlic, finely chopped

1 good bunch parsley, finely chopped

1 handful basil, finely chopped

salt and freshly ground black pepper

olive oil

a little vinegar

a little grated lemon peel

Combine all the ingredients. Make 5–6 hours in advance

•

To serve with bollito misto.

HORSERADISH SAUCE
SALSA DI RAFANO

115g/4oz grated fresh horseradish

115g/4oz fresh breadcrumbs, soaked in milk and squeezed dry

pinch of salt and a little sugar

300ml/½pt single cream

1 teaspoon vinegar

Combine all the ingredients.

•

To serve with bollito misto.

MOSTARDA DI VENEZIA

MAKES 1.6KG/3½LB
STORES FOR 1 YEAR IN A COOL PLACE

2kg/4½lb quinces

juice and zest of 1 lemon

200g/7oz sugar

4 tablespoons mustard powder

250g/9oz candied citron peel, minced

Peel, core and chop the quince, put the fruit in a saucepan with enough water to cover. Add the juice and zest of the lemon. Stir in half the sugar and bring to a simmer. Cook until the fruit is soft. Remove the fruit from the pan with a perforated spoon and place in a food processor. Add the remaining sugar and the mustard, dissolved in a little boiling water and made into a paste, to the pan. Stir and simmer gently until the liquid is reduced by about half and of a good syrupy consistency. Add a little syrup to the processor and blend. If the purée is too thick, add more liquid. The final consistency should be similar to apple sauce. Stir in the minced candied citron peel. Bottle in sterilized jars.

•

MOSTARDA DI CREMONA *Mostarda di Cremona consists of different candied fruits preserved in a mustard flavoured syrup. It is both sweet and hot. In Lombardy this is the classic accompaniment to bollito misto. It is widely obtainable from Italian delicatessens.*

PORCHETTA

Porchetta is the diminutive of porco, *meaning pig. A porchetta is a pig which is halfway between a full grown pig and a suckling pig. In the area round Macerata on the east coast of central Italy, where this dish comes from, you can buy porchetta in every village and town. It is made for robust people, not weight watchers! The aroma of the garlic and herbs as the hot crackling pig is put on the wooden tables in the butchers' shops is very tempting. Generally porchetta is eaten with unsalted bread. The farmers still keep their outside ovens to cook their porchettas in on special feast days. They stuff them with a certain type of wild fennel, the provenance of which is a feverishly guarded secret.*

SERVES APPROXIMATELY 18–20

1 small pig weighing about 12kg/26lb

salt

a little olive oil

Stuffing

good handful of rosemary

good handful of fennel fronds

1 head garlic, peeled

5 fillets pork

liver of the pig, chopped

salt and roughly ground black pepper

•

Liberally season with salt the inside of the deboned pig (ask your butcher to do this for you, and take home the meat trimmings).

•

Chop up the herbs and garlic coarsely and put it with the whole pork fillets and trimmings along the cavity. Scatter the chopped liver over as well.

•

Sew up the pig, place it sewn-side down on an oiled roasting tray and liberally season the outside with salt. Roast the porchetta for 1 hour in an oven set at 250°C/475°F/gas 9 then reduce the heat to 190°C/375°F/gas 5 and cook for a further 30 minutes. After about the first 40 minutes of cooking, or when the pig is golden brown and brown juices have formed in the tin, add 600ml/1pt of water to the roasting tray. Do not allow any water to get on top of the pig—the steam from the water will help to crisp the skin. Watch that the juices do not dry up; if necessary, keep topping up with water but do not baste during cooking.

•

Skim the fat from the rich juices and serve as a sauce. When the porchetta is cooked leave it to rest for 15 minutes before cutting. Cut into 1.5cm/¾in slices and serve with homemade bread and a salad. Potatoes roasted in extra-virgin olive oil, rosemary, garlic and salt also go well with porchetta.

FILLET OF PORK WITH CAPER FRUITS
FILETTO DI MAIALE E FRUTTI DI CAPPERI

SERVES 4

750g/1½lb fillet of pork

40g/1½oz butter

200ml/6fl oz brown stock

150ml/¼pt white wine

2 tablespoons caper fruits (or 2 tablespoons salted capers, well washed and dried)

salt and freshly ground white pepper

Cut the pork fillets into medallions 1½cm/½in thick.

•

In a frying pan, heat half the butter. When it is foaming, add the pork and fry until brown, 2 minutes on either side. Season with salt and pepper. Remove the medallions from the pan and keep warm. Deglaze the pan with the wine and reduce by two-thirds. Add the stock, bring to the boil, and strain the sauce into a small pan. Add the rest of the butter and the caper fruits. Pour the caper fruit sauce over the medallions and serve.

VEAL CUTLET TOURNOI

SERVES 4

4 veal cutlets

4 thin slices pâté de foie gras

1 truffle, thinly sliced

225g/½lb button mushrooms, sliced

butter

flour

salt and freshly ground black pepper

Sauce

1 cup veal stock

1 small glass Marsala

5 tablespoons double cream

small bunch of chervil

Split the veal cutlets and insert the slices of pâté de foie gras and a few slivers of truffle.

●

Season the cutlets and lightly dip in flour. Fry the cutlets gently in butter in a heavy-based frying pan. Fry until golden brown and cooked through. Place the cutlets on a serving dish and keep them warm.

●

Fry the mushrooms in a knob of butter. Reserve the mushrooms in a warm place.

●

Add a cup of veal stock and a small glass of Marsala to the frying pan in which the cutlets were cooked. Reduce the sauce slightly. Add the double cream and allow to thicken slightly. Season.

●

Place the mushrooms on top of the cutlets. Strain the sauce over the cutlets and sprinkle with finely chopped chervil.

Veal Escalope Bolognese

SCALLOPINA ALLA BOLOGNESE

SERVES 4

4 veal escalopes, lightly pounded

4 slices Parma ham

90g/3oz freshly grated Parmesan

3 tablespoons olive oil

1 egg lightly beaten with salt and freshly ground black pepper

dry fine breadcrumbs

butter (optional)

Dip the escalopes in beaten egg, then dredge in breadcrumbs. Press the breadcrumbs into the escalopes with the palm of the hand.

•

Heat the oil in a large frying pan and fry the escalopes until lightly browned on both sides. Reduce the heat, place a slice of Parma ham on top of each escalope and then sprinkle the Parmesan on top, to cover the ham. Place a lid on the pan and leave for a few minutes until the cheese has melted. Serve with a little melted butter over the top if you like; although correct, it is not necessary. This recipe can also be made with chicken or turkey breast.

Turkey Escalope with Marsala
SCALLOPINA DI TACCHINO CON MARSALA

SERVES 4

4 escalopes turkey

flour

1 wine glass Marsala

1 cup stock

1 tablespoon lemon juice

salt and freshly ground black pepper

olive oil and butter

Beat the escalopes gently with a meat basher between 2 sheets of greaseproof paper to make them larger and thinner. Dip the escalopes in flour and shake off any excess.

•

Heat a little oil and butter in a frying pan and when frothing put in the escalopes; brown them quickly on both sides. Season with salt and pepper and add lemon juice. Add the Marsala wine and let it bubble, then pour in the stock. Stir the sauce so the wine and stock are well amalgamated. Reduce the heat and let the contents of the pan simmer a minute or two, or until the sauce begins to turn syrupy.

•

Serve with mashed potatoes and an orange and chicory salad. Chicken breasts can be done in the same way.

TURKEY "OSSOBUCO"

SERVES 6

3 × 750g/1½lb turkey drumsticks, each cut through the bone into quarters (it is better to chill the drumsticks before sawing through with a junior hack saw)

flour

6 tablespoons olive oil

750g/1½lb ripe plum tomatoes, peeled, deseeded and chopped

1 glass dry white wine

salt and freshly ground black pepper

Gremolata

2½ teaspoons grated lemon peel

1 scant teaspoon finely chopped garlic

2½ tablespoons finely chopped parsley

Remove the large sinews and small bones from the drumsticks with kitchen pincers. Dust the pieces of turkey in flour. In a frying pan, fry the turkey pieces in olive oil until golden. Stir in the tomatoes and add the white wine, salt and freshly ground black pepper to taste. Cover the frying pan with a lid, reduce the flame and gently simmer for 30–40 minutes. Check the seasoning. The sauce should be reduced to a glaze.

•

Combine all the ingredients for the gremolata.

•

Put two turkey pieces on each plate, cover with the sauce and sprinkle gremolata on the top. Serve the turkey with mashed potatoes and a simple mixed green salad.

Breast of Chicken Périgourdine

PANTOUFLE PÉRIGOURDINE

SERVES 4

4 skinned breasts of chicken, wing tips removed

4 thin slices pâté de foie gras

flour

4 tablespoons clarified butter

salt and freshly ground white pepper

Périgourdine sauce

300ml/½pt rich chicken or veal stock

2 tablespoons brandy

4 tablespoons Madeira

1 black truffle, peeled and sliced

knob of butter

finely chopped parsley for garnish

Split the chicken breasts open and stuff with the pâté de foie gras. Seal the breast together using wooden cocktail sticks. Dust the breasts in flour and shake off the excess. Heat the clarified butter and gently cook the breasts until they are cooked through and golden all over. It will take 10–12 minutes. Season with salt and freshly ground white pepper.

•

Remove the breasts from the pan and keep warm. Add the brandy to the frying pan, flame it and add the Madeira. Reduce by half. Add the stock and reduce again by half. The sauce should have a shiny appearance. Sieve the sauce and keep warm.

•

Gently cook the truffle in a little butter.

•

Serve the pantoufle with the sauce poured over and slices of truffle arranged on top. Sprinkle with finely chopped parsley.

•

This supreme of chicken is called pantoufle because the finished supreme looks a little like an old-fashioned slipper.

Breast of Chicken with Radicchio, Mozzarella and Parma Ham

PETTO DI POLLO CON RADICCHIO, MOZZARELLA E PROSCIUTTO DI PARMA

SERVES 4

4 boneless breasts chicken, skin and wing tips removed

4 slices Parma ham

4 radicchio leaves

1 mozzarella, cut into quarters

1 egg, beaten and seasoned with salt and freshly ground black pepper

flour

dried breadcrumbs

olive oil for deep-frying

tomato coulis (page 107)

Split the breasts, remove the fillet and flatten out the breast and fillet between 2 sheets of grease-proof paper. Cover each breast with a slice of Parma ham, a radicchio leaf and a quarter of mozzarella, and cover with the fillet. Roll the breast up and seal with a little egg wash. Dust the breast with flour, then dip in the egg wash and finally roll in the breadcrumbs.

•

Deep-fry in olive oil for 10–12 minutes. The oil must not be too hot or the breadcrumbs will cook before the meat. This is the time when only personal judgement can be used, according to the equipment one is using. The breadcrumbs should be golden brown.

•

Serve with 2 tablespoons of tomato coulis on each plate with the chicken breast cut in half diagonally on top. The mozzarella should ooze out showing the colours of the ham and radicchio.

Poussin Stuffed with Grapes

SERVES 4

4 poussins (quails can also be cooked this way)

salt and freshly ground black pepper

1 glass dry white wine

60g/2oz seedless green grapes (seedless muscat grapes are recommended)

Stuffing

1 small onion, finely chopped

4 cloves garlic, finely chopped

6 tablespoons melted butter

115g/4oz seedless green grapes

1 tablespoon finely chopped parsley

2 tablespoons finely chopped sage

salt and freshly ground black pepper

1 thick slice day-old bread, made into breadcrumbs

First prepare the stuffing. Fry the onion and garlic in a little of the butter until golden. Remove from the heat and add the rest of the stuffing ingredients. Mix well together.

•

Season the inside of the birds with salt, and stuff each bird with the prepared stuffing. Truss the birds and rub with butter. Season with salt and pepper. Roast the poussins in a moderate oven 180°C/350°F/gas 4 for approximately 40 minutes, depending on the size of the birds. Baste from time to time with a little dry white wine. Skim the fat off the cooking juices before serving.

•

Add the grapes to the cooking juices 5 minutes before serving. Serve the poussins with a little of the cooking juices and a few grapes poured round them.

Roast Quail with Sage
QUAGLIE ARROSTO CON SALVIA

SERVES 4

8 plump quails

100g/3½oz butter

8 slices streaky bacon

8 sprigs sage

salt and freshly ground black pepper

lemon wedges

Salt and pepper the quails, stuff each one with a sprig of sage and put a little butter inside each cavity. Spread the rest of the butter on the breasts and legs of the birds. Wrap the streaky bacon around each bird making sure the thighs of the bird are covered. Place the quails in a roasting tin and roast in an oven set at 200°C/400°F/gas 6 for 15 minutes.

•

Remove the birds from the roasting tin. Serve with lemon wedges.

•

Crostoni (large slices of crusty bread fried in olive oil) spread with the lentils on page 171 are a nice accompaniment to the quails.

Quails in Potacchio
QUAGLIE IN POTACCHIO

SERVES 4

8 quails

2 tablespoons extra-virgin olive oil

6 plum tomatoes, peeled, seeded and chopped

1½ glasses dry white wine

1½ glasses water

24 cloves garlic, unpeeled

2 sprigs rosemary

In a large frying pan, fry the quails in the olive oil until golden. Add the chopped tomatoes and continue frying them for a few minutes. Be careful not to let the tomatoes catch.

•

Pour in the wine and water, add the unpeeled garlic and rosemary. If a light flavour of rosemary is preferred, the rosemary can be removed after 5 minutes. Cook the quails for 20 minutes or until they are cooked. The sauce should be well reduced.

•

Serve the quails with the sauce poured over and the garlic cloves. To eat the garlic, press the garlic cloves with the back of a fork and the flesh will easily come out of the skin. Less delicately, there is nothing nicer than picking them up and squeezing the succulent flesh into one's mouth … finger bowls are an absolute must!

•

In potacchio *is a style of cooking peculiar to the Marche region; the word comes from the French word* potage. *This method can also be used for chicken, rabbit or lamb (cut into quail-sized pieces). For lamb and rabbit omit the tomatoes.*

DUCK IN SWEET AND SOUR SAUCE
ANITRA IN AGRO DOLCE

SERVES 4

1 duck, weighing 2kg/4–5lb

2 large onions, finely sliced

30g/1oz butter

3 tablespoons chopped mint

2 large tablespoons of sugar

2 tablespoons white wine vinegar

pinch of ground cloves

450ml/¾pt chicken stock or duck stock

flour

salt and freshly ground black pepper

olive oil

Portion the duck into 4 pieces. Sweat the onions in the butter and transfer to a casserole. Season the duck portions with salt and pepper and dip in flour. Shake off excess flour and fry the duck portions in oil. When golden brown transfer to the casserole.

•

Add the cloves and season with salt and pepper. Cover the duck pieces with heated stock. Cover the casserole and bring to the boil, then lower the heat and gently simmer for 2 hours, more if necessary.

•

When the duck pieces are cooked, remove them from the sauce and keep warm in the oven. Skim off all the fat from the sauce and stir in the 3 tablespoons of chopped mint.

•

Caramelize the sugar until it is a dark caramel colour. Stir the caramelized sugar into the sauce and add the vinegar. Reduce the sauce until thickened and syrupy. Skim off the fat and check the seasoning.

•

Serve the duck with the sauce poured over it.

•

This is an adaptation of a recipe from Elizabeth David's Italian Food.

Roast Wild Duck and Kumquats

SERVES 4

2 wild ducks (if wild ducks are not available 2 Gressingham or Barbary ducks can be used instead)

salt

butter

2 tablespoons Grand Marnier

salt and freshly ground black pepper

watercress to garnish

Sauce

1 small onion, finely chopped

1 small carrot, finely chopped

1 tablespoon olive oil

3 tomatoes, peeled and chopped

450ml/¾pt veal stock (or chicken stock)

1 bouquet garni

175g/6oz sugar

150ml/¼pt white wine vinegar

20 kumquats, left whole

Before starting to cook the ducks, prepare the sauce. Fry the onion and carrot in olive oil until lightly browned, add the tomatoes and cook for a few minutes more. Add the stock and the bouquet garni, and simmer for 30 minutes, skimming regularly.

•

In another saucepan, melt the sugar very slowly until it begins to take on a little colour. Add the vinegar and stir over a low heat—the sugar may go hard, but keep on stirring and it will melt again. Strain the sauce onto this mixture and cook until the sauce is syrupy. Reserve.

•

Lightly salt the wild ducks and put a knob of butter inside the cavity of the bird. Cover the birds with butter and roast them in a hot oven 220°C/425°F/gas 7 for 20 minutes. Wild ducks should not be well done. Leave to rest for 10 minutes.

•

Add the kumquats to the sauce and warm through. Cut the ducks into serving pieces and put on a large serving dish. Sprinkle with the Grand Marnier and spoon over the kumquat sauce. Garnish with watercress and serve immediately with any extra sauce in a sauceboat.

WILD PIGEON WITH BRAISED LENTILS
PALOMBACCE CON LENTICCHE STUFATE

SERVES 4

4 wild pigeons

100g/3½oz bacon

1 onion

1 carrot

2 cloves garlic, crushed

1 bay leaf

1 sprig thyme

1 glass dry white wine

100g/3½oz tomato purée

1 litre/1¾pt water

6 tablespoons extra-virgin olive oil

salt and freshly ground black pepper to taste

braised lentils (page 171)

Finely chop the bacon, onion and carrot and fry in 3 tablespoons of the olive oil. Add the garlic, bay leaf, thyme and white wine, and transfer the vegetables to a heavy casserole.

•

Fry the pigeons in the rest of the olive oil and add them to the vegetables. Reduce the wine by four-fifths and add the tomato purée, diluted with 1 litre/1¾pt of water. Season with salt and freshly ground black pepper. Bring the sauce to the boil, cover the casserole and reduce the flame. Cook gently for 1–1½ hours. If the sauce reduces too much, add a little water.

•

Serve the pigeons with the sauce strained over them and the braised lentils.

Roast Partridge served on Croutons
PERNICE ARROSTO SUL CROSTONE

Place a knob of butter in the cavity of each bird and spread the remaining butter over the breasts and legs of the birds. Wrap the birds in the streaky bacon.

•

Preheat the oven to 220°C/425°F/gas 7. Place the birds breast-side up on a grid in a roasting tin and roast for 20 minutes. When the bacon starts to brown turn the birds over. Remove the bacon 5 minutes before the end of cooking time, and only at this point salt the bird.

•

Sauté the livers in butter until pink, season with thyme, mace, salt and pepper. Mash the livers with a fork.

•

Spread the liver mixture on 4 crostoni, and place the birds on top. Deglaze the roasting tin with a measure of brandy, flame, add the stock and reduce till slightly thickened. Strain the sauce and pour over the partridges. Serve the partridges with lemon wedges.

SERVES 4

4 partridges

200g/7oz butter

8 slices unsmoked streaky bacon

livers from the birds plus 2 chicken livers

large knob of butter (for frying livers)

pinch of mace

pinch of thyme

salt and freshly ground black pepper

1 measure brandy

1 cup chicken stock

lemon wedges

4 crostoni (large slices of country bread fried in olive oil)

GROUSE WITH BRANDY

SERVES 4

4 young grouse

225g/8oz butter

sprigs of fresh thyme

salt and freshly ground black pepper

8 rashers streaky bacon

1 cup strong chicken stock

1 glass brandy (or whisky)

4 croûtons, 7.5×5cm/3×2in, fried in butter

watercress and game chips to serve

redcurrant jelly

Singe any feathers remaining on the grouse. Be careful that the liver, which should have been left inside by your game supplier, does not drop out. Place the grouse in a roasting tin. Season inside the cavity. Put a knob of butter and a sprig of thyme inside the cavity as well. Season the outside of the grouse. Cover the breasts with the remaining butter. Wrap 2 rashers of bacon round the birds, tucking the ends in well underneath and making sure the thighs of the grouse are well covered.

•

Roast the birds in a preheated oven 200°C/400°F/gas 6 for about 20 minutes, basting regularly. A grouse should not be well done. Medium cooking is good, but some people prefer it rare. Remove the grouse from the roasting pan and leave them to rest in a warm place.

•

Pour off the fat from the roasting pan and add the stock. Add the warmed brandy; tilt the pan to ignite the alcohol. Scrape all the pan juices into the sauce.

•

Fry the croûtons in butter until golden brown.

•

Place a croûton on each plate, holding the grouse over the croûton, remove the thyme and with a fork remove the liver and gently mash it onto the croûton. Place the bird on top of the croûton.

•

When the flames of the sauce have subsided, strain the sauce over the birds.

•

Garnish with watercress and game chips. Serve with redcurrant jelly. If desired, bread sauce and buttered breadcrumbs are also delicious with grouse.

•

GROUSE *Young grouse should never be well cooked. We like to serve grouse cooked medium but some people prefer them rare; 15–20 minutes is ample for young birds, possibly a little longer as the season progresses and the birds get plumper. Grouse are good if hung for 5 days but can be hung up to 10 days if weather conditions permit. It is best cooked in the traditional British way. The Italians just love grouse and come over especially for the season.*

BUTTERED BREADCRUMBS

Melt the butter in a frying pan, add the breadcrumbs, season with salt and freshly ground white pepper. Fry the breadcrumbs until they are golden and crisp. Drain on absorbent kitchen paper and serve with roast game.

SERVES 4

60g/2oz day-old white breadcrumbs

30g/1oz butter

salt and freshly ground white pepper

BREAD SAUCE

SERVES 4–6

1 small onion

½ litre/¾pt milk

3 cloves

1 clove garlic

1 blade mace

1 bay leaf

6 whole peppercorns

2 allspice berries

60g/2oz day-old white breadcrumbs

2 tablespoons butter

salt

2 tablespoons cream

To serve with roast game.

Stick the cloves into the onion. Put the milk into a saucepan and add the onion, garlic, mace, bay leaf, peppercorns and allspice. Simmer the milk and spices for 15 minutes and leave to infuse for 1 hour.

Strain the milk over the breadcrumbs, add the butter and salt, and stir into the mixture. Return the sauce to the heat and cook over a gentle heat for 15 minutes, stirring occasionally. Add the cream, check the seasoning and serve at once.

Roast Woodcock

Woodcock is a very prized species of game. It is a small bird and the dark flesh has a decidedly strong wild flavour. Allow the birds to hang for 3–4 days. Woodcock are not usually drawn and should be served medium to rare after 10–20 minutes cooking at the most.

•

Brush the woodcock with the melted butter. Wrap 2 rashers of streaky bacon around each bird. Roast the woodcock in an oven set at 200°C/400°F/gas 6, for 10–20 minutes (rare or medium).

•

Place the toasted croûtons under the birds 5 minutes into the cooking time to catch the trail as it drops out. Before the birds are cooked, remove the bacon, baste the birds and return to the oven to brown.

•

Remove the roasting pan from the oven, season the birds with salt and freshly ground black pepper. Place the pan on a high heat, pour over the warmed brandy and set it alight. Let the flames die out and serve at once. A simple accompaniment of watercress and game chips is all that is necessary.

SERVES 4

4 woodcock

115g/4oz butter, melted

8 rashers streaky bacon

salt and pepper

2 spirit measures brandy

4 croûtons

SALMÌ OF HARE
LEPRE IN SALMÌ

SERVES 4

1 medium-sized hare

200g/7oz cultivated mushrooms

150g/5oz streaky bacon, diced

extra-virgin olive oil

200g/7oz finely chopped shallot

1 bunch parsley

1 bay leaf

1 sprig thyme

1 wine glass brandy

pinch of allspice

1 clove garlic, finely chopped

1 bottle red wine

salt, 6 black peppercorns and freshly ground black pepper

flour

Skin the hare, reserving the blood in a bowl (your game dealer will do this for you). Add a few tablespoons of red wine to the blood so that it does not coagulate. Reserve the liver in a little red wine as well.

•

Wash the hare, and joint it, place the joints in a deep bowl, add the chopped shallot, parsley, bay leaf, thyme, a pinch of salt and the black peppercorns, pour over the brandy and two glasses of red wine, and leave to marinate for 24 hours.

•

Heat 2 tablespoons of olive oil in a casserole and fry the diced bacon. When cooked, remove from the pan with a slotted spoon and reserve.

•

Drain the hare pieces from the marinade and dry them, then dust them with flour. Add 3 tablespoons more of olive oil to the casserole and fry the pieces of hare, add 2 glasses of red wine and the marinade, and season with salt and pepper, allspice and the finely chopped clove of garlic. Bring the sauce to the boil, cover the pan, lower the heat and gently simmer for 1½–2 hours, or until the hare is cooked.

•

Slice the mushrooms and fry in 2 tablespoons of olive oil. Reserve.

•

When the pieces of hare are cooked, remove them to a clean casserole, add the mushrooms and bacon, strain the sauce over the meat pieces and keep warm. A few minutes before serving, add the blood and the liver of the hare cut in thin slices. This last process can be omitted. Check the seasoning. Serve the hare with polenta, tagliatelle or creamed potato.

Wild Boar Chops in Sweet and Sour Sauce
COSTOLETTE DI CINGHIALE IN AGRO DOLCE

SERVES 4

4 wild boar chops

a little olive oil

1 tablespoon finely chopped candied citron peel

¼ cup pine kernels

salt and freshly ground black pepper

Sauce

8 tablespoons sugar

8 bay leaves

2 cups red wine vinegar

175g/6oz sultanas

175g/6oz bitter chocolate

175g/6oz prunes (prunes d'Agen are best)

pinch of freshly grated nutmeg

To make the sauce. Put the sugar, bay leaves and vinegar in a pan over a low heat and stir until the sugar is dissolved. Reduce the sauce to a light syrup. Add the sultanas, bitter chocolate and a pinch of nutmeg. Stir the sauce gently until the chocolate has melted. Add the prunes, which should have been stoned.

•

Season the chops and either grill or fry them in a little olive oil till they are just cooked through.

•

Leave them to rest for 5 minutes. To serve, pour the sauce over the chops and sprinkle the candied citron cubes and pine kernels on top of the cutlets.

GUINEA FOWL COOKED IN CLAY

FARAONA ALLA CRETA

SERVES 4

1 guinea fowl, weighing about 1½kg/3½lb

4 slices Parma ham

butter

2 sprigs each of sage, thyme and rosemary

salt and freshly ground white pepper

clay (about 1.1kg/2½lb)

About 1.1kg/2½lb of clay is needed to cover the bird. Make sure that the thickness of the clay is the same all round and that there are no holes or weak spots. Cooking in clay is a very old method of cooking.

In the mid 1960s, they were building houses in the village near us. Franco found a seam of clay and every day would go to fetch some to cook chickens and guinea fowl, or even quails, in this way. Clay can be bought from your local pottery—it is easier!

•

Dampen a sheet of rough brown wrapping paper place a sheet of greaseproof paper on top. Put the guinea fowl on the greaseproof, and stuff the bird with the herbs and a large knob of butter. Spread butter over the breast and thighs of the bird and wrap the four slices of Parma ham round it. Season with salt and freshly ground white pepper. Parcel the bird up well, first the greaseproof, then the wrapping paper, and cover all over with a layer of clay about 1cm/½in thick.

•

Preheat the oven 250°C/475°F/gas 9. Put the guinea fowl on a roasting tray into the oven and cook for 2½ hours.

•

Remove the bird from the oven and break the clay with a hammer.

"Coal-pot" Guinea Fowl

In the West Indies, where this dish came from, the guinea fowl would be cooked in a coal-pot, hence the name. A coal-pot is a terracotta brazier with a butt (casserole) which fits on top of coals. The brazier is also used for barbecuing food. Do not be put off if you have not got a coal-pot. A heavy casserole on a gas or electric stove is just as good. Note the sugar and oil method of frying which is very common in the West Indies.

SERVES 4

- *2 medium-sized guinea fowl*
- *2 teaspoons vinegar*
- *2 cloves garlic, chopped*
- *1 tablespoon each of finely chopped parsley, thyme and celery leaves*
- *2 tablespoons chopped spring onion*
- *1 teaspoon salt*
- *½ teaspoon freshly ground black pepper*
- *2 tablespoons light rum*
- *2 teaspoons brown sugar*
- *¼ cup corn oil*

●

Joint the guinea fowl. Blend together all the other ingredients, except the sugar and oil, and marinate the bird for at least one hour.

●

Heat the oil in a heavy pot, add the sugar to the hot oil and allow to caramelize. Remove the guinea fowl from the marinade and drain well. Add the pieces to the oil and sugar which should be nicely browned. Stir and turn the pieces of fowl until they are browned all over.

●

Add the marinade and enough water just to cover the pieces of guinea fowl. Season with salt and pepper. Cover the pot and gently cook for about 40 minutes. The sauce should be reduced by about two-thirds. Correct the seasoning. Serve with plain boiled brown lentils.

Pheasant with Chestnuts and Onions
FAGIANO CON CIPOLLE E CASTAGNE

SERVES 4

2 hen pheasants

60g/2oz butter

200g/7oz pearl onions

200g/7oz chestnuts, boiled and peeled

15g/½oz flour

600ml/1pt chicken stock

30g/1oz redcurrant jelly

3 strips orange peel and the juice of 1 orange

1 tablespoon wine vinegar

1 bay leaf

salt and freshly ground black pepper

2 tablespoons finely chopped parsley

Portion the pheasants into quarters.

•

Melt half the butter in a frying pan, and when it is foaming, add the pheasant portions and fry until golden all over. Transfer the pheasant portions to a casserole.

•

Peel the pearl onions and fry them in 15g/½oz of butter until golden. Reserve.

•

To the pan in which the onions were cooked, add the rest of the butter and the flour. Stir the flour into the butter and let it cook gently for 5 minutes until it is a golden colour. Add the stock and bring to the boil.

•

Add the redcurrant jelly, the orange peel, orange juice and the wine vinegar to the stock. Mix the sauce with a balloon whisk to ensure there are no lumps. Pour the sauce over the pheasants.

•

Add the bay leaf, cover the casserole and put in an oven set at 180°C/350°F/gas 4. Cook for 1 hour. Forty minutes into the cooking time add the onions.

•

Remove the pheasant to a warm dish and season the pieces with salt and freshly ground black pepper.

•

Reduce the sauce over a high heat for 5 minutes, and then season with salt and freshly ground black pepper. Toss the chestnuts in 15g/½oz of butter until golden and add to the sauce.

●

Serve the pheasant with the sauce, onions and chestnuts poured over. Sprinkle with chopped parsley.

●

As an accompaniment, serve either chestnut tagliatelle (page 86) or chestnut gnocchi tossed in melted butter (page 117).

Guinea Fowl with Vin Santo, Chanterelles and Spinach

SERVES 4

4 breasts guinea fowl

250g/9oz chanterelles

200g/7oz spinach

100ml/3½fl oz Vin Santo

600ml/1pt rich guinea fowl stock

70g/2½oz butter

15g/½oz sultanas

1 tablespoon pine kernels

knob of butter

salt and freshly ground black pepper

Macerate the sultanas in the Vin Santo. Make a rich stock from the bones of the guinea fowl. Reduce the Vin Santo from the sultanas down to almost nothing, add the stock and cook briskly for about 15 minutes. Strain the sauce.

•

Fry the breasts of guinea fowl in 40g/1½oz of butter until golden on both sides, season with salt and freshly ground black pepper. Put them in a hot oven for 10 minutes. Remove the breasts from the oven and leave them to rest for 10 minutes.

•

Cook the spinach with a little salt—water is not necessary—and drain well. In a pan, melt the rest of the butter and add the spinach, salt and pepper, pine kernels and sultanas. Stir the butter in well.

•

Fry the chanterelles in a knob of butter. Season with salt and pepper.

•

Divide the spinach between 4 plates, place a breast of guinea fowl, sliced in 4 across the breast, on top of the spinach and cover with the sauce. Surround the guinea fowl with the mushrooms.

•

When buying the breasts of guinea fowl ask for them to be left on the bone. Debone them yourself and use the bones to make the rich stock. If you have whole birds use the legs for making a pie or casserole.

Pheasant Cacciatora with Olives
FAGIANO ALLA CACCIATORA CON OLIVE

SERVES 4

2 hen pheasants, quartered

6 cloves garlic, finely chopped

6 tablespoons extra-virgin olive oil

salt and freshly ground black pepper

1 glass dry white wine

4 tablespoons white wine vinegar

80 black olives, pitted

4 anchovies

24 caper fruit, marinated in white wine vinegar

Cut the pheasants in 4 portions.

•

In a large cocotte, fry the finely chopped garlic in two tablespoons of olive oil, and reserve.

•

Fry the pheasant portions in the remaining oil until deep golden. Return the garlic and oil to the cocotte, and season the pheasants with salt and freshly ground black pepper. Add the wine and vinegar plus the olives, half left whole, the rest chopped finely. Finally add the anchovies, mashed with a fork, and a glass of water. Lower the heat and cover the cocotte. Cook gently until the birds are tender and the sauce reduced. Serve with the sauce poured over and the caper fruit scattered on top.

•

If caper fruit are not available use well-washed salted capers.

Pork and Liver Sausage
SALSICCE DI FEGATO

MAKES APPROXIMATELY 32 SAUSAGES

1.4kg/3lb pork shoulder

450g/1lb pigs liver

grated rind of ¼ orange, blanched

60g/2oz salt

14g/½oz freshly coarsely ground black pepper

2 cloves garlic, crushed

2 pinches grated nutmeg

2 pinches allspice

sausage casings (obtainable from butchers)

60ml/2fl oz dry white wine at room temperature

wine for soaking casings

Mince the pork and liver, add all the other ingredients and mix well. Soak the casings in wine for 5 minutes and using a sausage maker with a standard nozzle make the sausages.

•

These sausages have a 20-day life hanging in the fridge. Prick the sausages and hang in a cool dry place for 3 days before using them.

•

Fry the sausages in extra-virgin olive oil or split them in half and cook them on a barbecue. Serve with lentils or butter beans boiled and dressed with extra-virgin olive oil and garlic and seasoned with salt and pepper.

•

This recipe is characteristic of the central Marche. In the southern part of the Marche they use chilli pepper instead of ordinary pepper.

Pork Sausages
SALSICCE DI MAIALE MARCHIGIANE

Mince the pork, season with the salt, pepper, garlic and spices. Add the wine and mix together all the ingredients. Soak the casings in wine for 5 minutes, then using a sausage maker with a standard nozzle, make the sausages. Prick the sausages and hang them in a cool dry place. These sausages will keep for up to 30 days hanging in a fridge. Allow the sausages to hang for 3 days before using them.

•

Gently fry the sausages in a little extra-virgin olive oil, sufficient to cover the base of a frying pan. Turn the sausages over as they become golden brown, reduce the heat, place a lid on the frying pan and leave to cook for a few minutes, or until cooked through. When cooked, remove the sausages from the pan and keep them warm between two plates. To the oil in the frying pan, add a ½ glass of dry white wine and reduce by half. Add the tomato coulis with 1 cup of water and a pinch of oregano and boil the sauce for a few seconds.

•

Serve the sausages with the sauce poured over.

MAKES 18–20

1 kg/2¼lb pork shoulder, fat and lean

21g/¾oz salt

7g/¼oz freshly coarsely ground black pepper

2 cloves garlic, crushed

pinch of grated nutmeg

pinch of mixed allspice

30ml/1fl oz dry white wine at room temperature

sausage casings (available from butchers)

wine at room temperature to soak casings

SERVES 4

2–3 sausages per person

extra-virgin olive oil

½ glass dry white wine

1 cup tomato coulis (page 107) or sugo finto (page 171)

oregano

Cotechino

MAKES 3 × 300G/10 OZ APPROX.

500g/1lb 2oz pork shoulder

200g/7oz pork belly

300g/10oz pig skin

2 tablespoons salt

1 teaspoon mixed spices

¼ teaspoon saltpetre

1 clove garlic, crushed

sausage casings; the finished result should be 3 cotechino 5cm/2in wide × 20cm/8in long (available from butchers)

white wine

For the mixed spice, grind together:

1 tablespoon peppercorns

3–4 cloves

1 × 4cm/1½in piece cinnamon

pinch of nutmeg

2 pieces mace

2 dry bay leaves

pinch of dry thyme

Mince the meats, chop the skin finely and mix all the ingredients together. Soak the casings in wine for 5 minutes. Then stuff the mixture into the casings. A sausage maker is required for this operation.

•

Hang the cotechini in a dry, cool place and leave for 20 days at least before using. Don't allow the cotechini to touch each other.

•

To cook. Wrap the cotechino in a clean white napkin and tie it up. Place the cotechino in cold water and slowly bring it to the boil. Reduce the heat and boil gently. The time required is:

300g/10oz	1¾ hours
500g/1lb2oz	2 hours
1 kg/2½lb	3 hours

•

A cotechino weighing 300g/10oz serves 2 people. Serve it with these lentils opposite.

Lentils

SERVES 4

400g/14oz lentils (Puy or Cavelluchi)

90g/3½oz Parma ham, finely chopped

1 onion, finely chopped

1 stick celery, finely chopped

2 tablespoons extra-virgin olive oil

stock

salt and freshly ground black pepper

Soak the lentils overnight, drain and wash them, and check for stones. Fry the Parma ham in the olive oil with the onion and celery. When the vegetables are soft, add the lentils and stir in for a minute or two. Add enough hot stock to cover the lentils by 2.5cm/1in, and season with salt and freshly ground black pepper. Gently cook until the lentils are tender. This takes about half an hour but very much depends on the age of the lentils.

False Sauce
SUGO FINTO

SERVES 4

1 kg/2¼lb tomatoes, they must be very ripe, peeled, seeded and roughly chopped

100g/3½oz streaky bacon, diced

1 stalk of celery, finely diced

1 carrot, finely diced

½ onion, finely diced

1 clove garlic, finely chopped

1 glass dry white wine

1 tablespoon finely chopped parsley

1 generous pinch marjoram

salt and freshly ground black pepper

extra-virgin olive oil

In 2 tablespoons of olive oil, fry the bacon with the celery, carrot, onion and garlic and fry until the onion is golden. Add the wine and reduce it briskly over a high flame by two-thirds. Lower the heat, add the tomatoes, and the parsley, marjoram, salt and pepper. Leave the sauce to cook gently for 45 minutes. Pass the sauce through a sieve and serve with *salsicce marchigiane* (page 169). This sauce is also good on pasta, in which case do not sieve it.

CALVES' LIVER WITH SULTANAS AND BALSAMIC VINEGAR

FEGATO DI VITELLO ALL'UVA

SERVES 4

8 slices calves' liver weighing 100g/3½oz each

75g/2½oz butter

2 tablespoons golden sultanas, soaked in a little white wine

1 tablespoon tomato coulis (page 107)

4 tablespoons port

2 tablespoons brandy

20 drops balsamic vinegar

salt and freshly ground black pepper

In a frying pan large enough to take the 4 slices of liver, melt the butter and when it is foaming add the liver and cook until medium cooked, turning once. Season with salt and freshly ground black pepper.

•

Remove the liver from the pan, add the sultanas, tomato coulis, port and brandy. Mix well together to make a smooth sauce. Check the seasoning.

•

Serve the liver with the sauce poured over it.

Calves' Liver with Sweet and Sour Onions
FEGATO CON CIPOLLINE AGRO DOLCE

To make the sweet and sour onions, drop the onions in boiling water to make it easier to peel them. Place the peeled onions in fresh boiling water and boil for 5 minutes. Drain. Melt the butter in a saucepan, add the sugar and stir over a medium heat for a few minutes. Add the wine vinegar and continue to stir. Add the onions and stir well. Cover the pan and place in the oven at 160°C/325°F/gas 3 for about 10 minutes, or until golden.

•

Season the flour with salt and pepper and dust the liver. Heat a little oil in a frying pan and cook the liver for 3 minutes on each side. Remove the liver from the pan and keep warm. Throw away any oil left in the pan. Add the Marsala, sherry and stock and cook briskly until a glaze forms.

•

Pour this sauce over the liver and garnish with the onions and sage.

SERVES 4

8 thin slices calves' liver, 100g/3$\frac{1}{2}$oz each

flour (enough to dust the liver)

salt and freshly ground black pepper

extra-virgin olive oil

150ml/$\frac{1}{4}$pt Marsala

70ml/2$\frac{1}{2}$fl oz dry sherry

70ml/2$\frac{1}{2}$fl oz meat stock

sage for garnish

Sweet and sour onions

750g/1$\frac{3}{4}$lb baby onions

50g/2oz butter

30g/1$\frac{1}{4}$oz sugar

70ml/2$\frac{1}{2}$fl oz white wine vinegar

OXTAIL WITH WINE AND TOMATOES
CODA DI BUE ALLA VACCINARA

SERVES 6

1.6kg/$3\frac{1}{2}$lb oxtails

flour

6 tablespoons extra-virgin olive oil

1 large onion, finely chopped

3 carrots, finely chopped

3 cloves garlic, finely chopped

1 glass dry red wine

3 tablespoons tomato purée

small bunch of parsley

500g/1lb2oz plum tomatoes, peeled and chopped roughly

6 cloves

salt and freshly ground black pepper

Cut the oxtails into 5cm/2in pieces, trim off as much fat as possible and leave to soak in cold water for at least 4 hours. Drain, then rinse them under cold running water and dry thoroughly with a cloth. Dip the oxtails in flour, and shake off the surplus.

•

Fry the oxtails in olive oil until golden all over. Transfer the oxtails to a heavy casserole.

•

In fresh olive oil, fry the onion, carrot and garlic. When lightly browned, add the vegetables to the casserole. Add the wine and reduce down, then add the tomato purée and enough boiling water to cover the oxtails. Season with salt and pepper, add the cloves and parsley. Cover the casserole and leave to simmer for about 5 hours over a low heat.

•

During the cooking, stir the oxtails from time to time to make sure they do not stick.

•

One hour before the end of the cooking, add the peeled and chopped tomatoes.

•

Remove the casserole from the heat and skim off the fat. It is better to leave the oxtails to go cold overnight and then remove any fat which may be left. The oxtail sauce should be dense.

•

Serve with celery, chopped in 1cm/$\frac{1}{2}$in pieces, and boiled.

Lambs' Kidneys with Truffles and Marsala

ROGNONE DI AGNELLO AL MARSALA E TARTUFI

SERVES 4

450g/1lb lambs' kidneys

olive oil

150ml/¼pt Marsala

1 lemon

salt and freshly ground black pepper

2 black truffles, sliced (optional)

chopped parsley for garnish

fried bread triangles

Skin the kidneys and cut them in half. Plunge in boiling water with the juice of half a lemon. Leave them for a minute or two and then drain. Cut the kidneys into thin slices and cook them gently in 2 tablespoons of olive oil for about 3 minutes. Season with salt and freshly ground black pepper. Add the Marsala and let it bubble until reduced by half. Add a little lemon juice.

•

If using truffles, toss in now and serve the kidneys with parsley sprinkled on top and triangles of bread fried in olive oil.

SWEETBREADS WITH WILD MUSHROOMS AND MARSALA

ANIMELLE D'AGNELLO CON FUNGHI SELVATICI E MARSALA

SERVES 6

500g/1lb 2oz lambs' sweetbreads

150g/5oz Parma ham, cut in julienne

40g/1½oz butter

4 tablespoons olive oil

½ glass Marsala

250g/9oz mixed wild mushrooms, sliced (use cultivated if necessary)

salt and freshly ground black pepper

crostini (½cm/¼in slices of French bread fried in olive oil)

Leave the sweetbreads to soak for 10 minutes, drain and put in a pan of cold water and bring to the boil. After a minute, drain the sweetbreads and refresh them under cold water. Remove the skin and membranes and dry well.

•

Melt the butter and oil in a heavy pan, add the sweetbreads and fry briskly until lightly browned. Add the Parma ham, drain off as much fat as possible, pour over the Marsala and reduce rapidly until a glaze comes on the sauce.

•

Fry the wild mushrooms in oil, remove with a perforated spoon and add to the sweetbreads. Season with salt and pepper.

•

Serve with the crostini fried in olive oil.

TRIPE IN WINE
TRIPPA IN UMIDO

If the beans are dried, soak them in cold water overnight. Boil them in unsalted water, and salt after cooking. Buy calves' tripe ready blanched and check with your butcher how much longer it should be cooked. Cut the tripe into strips 1cm×10cm/½in×4in.

•

Fry the celery, onion, carrot and garlic in oil and butter until lightly golden. Add the tomatoes and fry until they have made a sauce. Add the tripe, season with salt and pepper, add the basil, and cook to the butcher's recommended time.

•

Cook on a low heat, covered, but check from time to time and if the sauce starts to get a bit dry, add a little water. Half way through the cooking add the tiny potatoes. Keep stirring the tripe every now and then to make sure it does not stick. Check the seasoning.

•

To serve, ladle the tripe into shallow soup bowls. Add the cooked butter beans and sprinkle with parsley and grated Parmesan cheese.

•

This dish is good reheated, and can be cooked the day before required. It keeps perfectly in the refrigerator. Fresh butter beans are available in the autumn from Middle Eastern shops.

SERVES 6

1kg/2¼lb calves' tripe

500g/1lb2oz tomatoes, peeled and chopped

300g/10oz butter beans, dried or fresh

1 stick celery, finely chopped

1 large onion, finely chopped

2 carrots, finely chopped

1 clove garlic, finely chopped

1 sprig basil

12 baby potatoes

2 tablespoons olive oil

50g/1½oz butter

1 bunch parsley, finely chopped

freshly grated Parmesan cheese

salt and freshly ground black pepper

Fish

Fish features strongly on our menu. This is because Franco's formative years were spent near Ancona on the Adriatic coast of Italy, where fish dominates the diet. Every kind of fish one can think of.

When we first came to Wales it was quite hard for us to find good fresh fish. Eventually we used to go and buy it ourselves straight from the boats in Solva (a beautiful natural harbour) in Pembrokeshire, or at Milford Haven and Haverfordwest on the west coast of Wales. On the way back we would stop at Llanstephan on the estuary, where the river Towy meets the sea. Here we would buy grey mullet, very often helping to pull the nets in. It was a long journey but worth it.

As the years passed, the fishermen started to deliver to us, but we still get pleasure from collecting cockles and samphire at Penclawdd on the Swansea estuary. We take the commis chefs with us, so they can see that cockles do not come in polythene bags off the fishmonger's slab. It is back-breaking, picking cockles, invariably in drizzly mist, but the joy of coming home with buckets of them, freshly sieved from the sand, makes up for it all. Or is it the fact we have survived another trip? There are signs at the top of the beach saying, "Unexploded mines!".

BRODETTO *This is the fish stew of the Marche. For centuries it was the dish of the fishermen to use up the fish not wanted by their customers. It evolved into a more refined but still robust dish over the years. There are many ways of preparing this dish and great arguments are to be heard as to which is the best—with saffron or without?, and so it goes on. Originally brodetto always had thirteen different types of fish, corresponding to the number of people who were present at the last supper. Less can be used, but never twelve as this is considered to be an unlucky number, reminding them of the traitor Judas.*

It is amusing to see the fish restaurants along the coastline with signs saying "Vincenzo il mago", the wizard of the brodetto, or "Carlo, il ré", the king of the brodetto! In fishing seaside resorts, like Porto Recanati, the fishermen are to be seen bringing their catch in very early in the morning and selling it directly to the housewives and chefs at the quayside or in their own shops. No housewife or chef buys fish after 10 o'clock in the morning and whatever is left is sold off cheaply. No tired fish there.

FISH CASSEROLE
BRODETTO

This is how we prepare brodetto.

Clean the fish and cut into largish chunks. Clean the mussels and prawns but do not shell the prawns. Discard any mussels that are damaged or open. Clean the squid and slice finely.

Fry the onion and garlic in olive oil in a shallow pan (preferably one with two handles) until golden. Add the squid to the pan and cook for 3–4 minutes. Stir in the chopped tomatoes, wine and a few drops of vinegar, the tomato coulis or passato and a little salted water to the pan. After a few minutes, add 2 tablespoons chopped parsley, then the prawns and the thicker pieces of fish. Leave to cook a few minutes, then add the remaining fish and the mussels. Cover the pan and cook over a medium heat until the fish is done, shaking the pan gently from time to time so that the fish does not stick. Remove the pan from the heat and leave to rest, covered with the lid, for 2–3 minutes.

Serve sprinkled with the rest of the parsley and bread toasted on the griddle.

SERVES 6

1.6kg/3½lb fish, a mixture of red mullet, monkfish, whiting, gurnard, sole, mussels and Dublin Bay prawns as available

425g/15oz squid

1 onion, very finely chopped

1 clove garlic, crushed

3 tablespoons extra-virgin olive oil

6 ripe plum tomatoes, peeled, seeded and chopped

150ml/¼pt dry white wine

white wine vinegar

425g/15oz plum tomato passato or coulis *(page 107)*

3 tablespoons finely chopped parsley

toasted country bread

BRODETTO OF SOLE, ANCONA-STYLE
BRODETTO DI SOGLIOLA ALL'ANCONETANA

SERVES 4

4 sole, weighing 400g/14oz each, skinned and filleted, bones and skin reserved

1 glass dry white wine

juice of ½ lemon

60ml/2fl oz extra virgin-olive oil

1 carrot

¼ onion

70g/2½oz finely chopped onion

2 cloves garlic, finely chopped

1 stick celery, finely chopped

200g/7oz tomato concassé (page 81)

pinch of saffron threads, in a little water

1 bouquet garni (2 sprigs parsley, 1 sprig thyme, 1 bay leaf)

16 slices French bread, toasted

1 tablespoon finely chopped parsley

salt and freshly ground black pepper

Put 1 litre/1¾ pints of cold water in a casserole with the wine, lemon juice, fish trimmings and bones, carrot and onion. Season with salt and pepper. Bring the stock to the boil, reduce the flame and simmer for half an hour. Sieve the stock and reserve.

•

In a large shallow pan, heat the oil and add the chopped onion, celery and garlic. When slightly golden, add the tomato concassé, saffron and bouquet garni. Leave the sauce to cook for a few minutes then add the fish stock. Boil the sauce gently for 15 minutes, then add the sole fillets which have been rolled up, and cook for a further 8–10 minutes over a high heat.

•

Toast the French bread slices. Put the fish and soup in shallow soup bowls, sprinkle the fish with parsley and garnish with toasted bread. This dish should be eaten with a spoon and fork.

Panaché of Fish with Warm Balsamic Vinaigrette

SERVES 6

1kg/2¼lb mixed fillets of Dover sole, sea bass, red mullet and brill

6 well-cleaned scallops, including coral

60g/2oz tomato concassé (page 81)

4 teaspoons finely chopped mixed fresh herbs such as chervil, tarragon, basil, chives

For the balsamic vinaigrette

1 clove garlic, crushed

70ml/2½fl oz extra-virgin olive oil

70ml/2½fl oz balsamic vinegar

salt and freshly ground black pepper

Season the fish and place in a steamer with the scallops. Cook until lightly done, 3–4 minutes.

•

Meanwhile, mix together the ingredients for the vinaigrette with salt and pepper to taste and warm up in a saucepan. When the fish is ready, transfer the fish to 4 warm dinner plates and pour the warm vinaigrette over but do not be too generous.

•

Decorate with tomato concassé (small dice) and the finely chopped fresh herbs. Serve immediately.

EEL IN WHITE WINE AND TOMATO
ANGUILLA IN UMIDO

SERVES 4

1kg/2½lb eel (fresh water)

3 tablespoons extra-virgin olive oil

20g/¾oz butter

1 clove garlic, finely chopped

30g/1oz finely chopped parsley

2 sage leaves

1 bay leaf

1 wine glass dry white wine

1 tablespoon tomato purée, dissolved in a glass of water

salt and freshly ground black pepper

Cut the eel into 7.5cm/3in pieces and fry in the oil and butter. Add the garlic, finely chopped parsley, sage, bay leaf, white wine, and tomato purée dissolved in a glass of water. Season the eel with salt and freshly ground black pepper. Gently cook for 15–20 minutes over a moderate heat. Serve with crostini.

SMALL SQUID WITH OLIVE OIL AND GARLIC
CALAMARETTI CON OLIO E AGLIO

SERVES 4

800g/1¾lb fresh tiny calamari (squid), cleaned

4 tablespoons extra-virgin olive oil

2 cloves garlic, finely chopped

juice of 1 lemon

dried chilli flakes

salt

30g/1oz finely chopped parsley

Gently heat the olive oil in a large frying pan. Add the garlic and let it colour slightly. Add the cleaned squid and stew gently over a low heat, turning regularly for 30 minutes. Halfway through the cooking, add a good pinch of chilli flakes and salt. At the last moment, add the parsley and lemon juice, stir in well. These squid can be eaten hot or cold.

Scallops Marinara
CAPESANTE ALLA MARINARA

SERVES 4

8 large scallops and 4 shells

1 clove garlic, finely chopped

2 tablespoons finely chopped parsley

2 tablespoons extra-virgin olive oil

salt and freshly ground black pepper

pinch of dried chilli pepper flakes

juice of ½ lemon

1 glass dry white wine

lemon wedges

Remove the greyish beard around the scallops, and also the blackish sac. Wash the scallops in plenty of cold water and dry on absorbent kitchen paper.

•

Heat the olive oil over a medium heat, add the garlic and 1 tablespoon parsley and fry for a few seconds. Add the scallops and sauté for a minute or two. Season with salt, pepper and chilli pepper. Remove the scallops from the pan.

•

Add the wine to the pan and reduce to a light syrup. Stir in the lemon juice and reduce a little. Return scallops to sauce and reheat.

•

To serve, put 2 scallops into each shell and pour the sauce over. Sprinkle with the rest of the chopped parsley. Serve at once with extra lemon wedges.

GRILLED RAZOR SHELLS
CANNELLO IN GRATELLA

SERVES 4

20 razor shells

1 cup white breadcrumbs

2 tablespoons finely chopped parsley

1 clove garlic, finely chopped

juice of ½ lemon

extra-virgin olive oil

salt and freshly ground black pepper

lemon wedges for serving

Leave the razor shells for 2–3 hours in salted tepid water. This is to remove the sand. Open the shells with a knife, cutting the valve. Discard the empty shell.

•

Mix the breadcrumbs, parsley, garlic, lemon juice, salt and pepper. Divide the mixture between the shells and sprinkle with extra-virgin olive oil. Place the razor shells under a medium grill and grill for 12–15 minutes. Serve with lemon wedges. Use also as part of antipasto di mare (page 56).

BROCHETTE OF GRILLED SCAMPI WRAPPED IN BACON
SPIEDINI DI SCAMPONI CON PANCETTA ALLA GRIGLIA

SERVES 4

32 large, fresh raw scampi

32 pieces of thinly sliced smoked streaky bacon

freshly ground black pepper

extra-virgin olive oil

lemon wedges for serving

Wash and peel the scampi, remove the grey sac. Wrap a piece of streaky bacon around each one. Thread 8 scampi onto 4 skewers. If using wooden skewers, soak them in water for at least 1 hour before using them. Sprinkle the scampi with a little extra-virgin olive oil. Place the skewers under the grill, turning them during the cooking. When the bacon is cooked, the scampi are ready. Serve with freshly ground black pepper sprinkled on top and wedges of lemon.

Grilled Scampi
SCAMPI ALLA GRIGLIA

Wash the scampi thoroughly and split them not quite through lengthways. Flatten and remove the grey sac. Mix the breadcrumbs, 4 tablespoons of the olive oil, garlic, parsley, chilli flakes, salt and freshly ground black pepper together. Cover the body part of the scampi with this mixture. Sprinkle the head part with Parmesan cheese. Sprinkle the rest of the oil over the scampi, place on the wire rack of the grill and grill for 10–12 minutes depending on size. When the flesh of the scampi looks milky it is cooked. Serve with lemon wedges.

SERVES 4

20 large raw scampi, shells left on (langoustines)

30g/1oz fresh white breadcrumbs

8 tablespoons extra-virgin olive oil

1 clove garlic, finely chopped

6 tablespoons finely chopped parsley

pinch of dried chilli flakes

salt and freshly ground black pepper

4 tablespoons freshly grated Parmesan cheese

lemon wedges for serving

Lobster with a Sauce of Vin Santo
ARAGOSTA CON SALSA DI VIN SANTO

SERVES 4

4 raw lobsters, each weighing 450g/1lb

60g/2oz sultanas

175ml/6fl oz Vin Santo (sweet sherry can be substituted)

100g/4oz butter

pinch of freshly grated nutmeg

salt and freshly coarsely ground white pepper

Marinate the sultanas in the Vin Santo for at least 1 hour.

•

Put the lobsters in boiling salted water and boil for 3 minutes. Turn the heat off and leave to stand for 5 minutes. Remove the lobsters from the water, cut in half and remove the stomach and sandbag. Crack the claws.

•

Melt the butter in a pan and add a small pinch of nutmeg, a little salt and plenty of freshly ground white pepper. When the butter is foaming, add the Vin Santo from the sultanas to the pan, cook until reduced by half, stirring from time to time. Add the sultanas. Pour the sauce over the prepared lobster.

•

Vin Santo is made from white grapes which are hung on racks during the winter. They shrivel and concentrate their sugar, and are then pressed during Easter Holy Week—hence its name.

Crab with Lemon Dressing
GRANCHI CON LIMONE

Bring a pan of water, large enough to hold the 4 crabs with plenty of room, to the boil. Season the water with the salt, peppercorns, bay leaves and lemon. Add the crabs upside down—so the claws will not break off—and bring the water back to the boil. Boil for 5 minutes, turn off the heat and leave the crabs in the water for 15 minutes, then plunge them into cold water, drain and leave to get cold.

•

Remove all the white meat from the body. Leave the brown meat inside the shell and be careful to discard the possibly poisonous dead men's fingers. These are gills which filter water, the purity of which cannot be guaranteed. Return the white meat to the body shell, crack the claw shells to expose the meat.

•

Make the dressing with the lemon juice, extra-virgin olive oil, chopped parsley, garlic and salt and freshly ground black pepper to taste. Mix ingredients with a fork to amalgamate well. Spoon the sauce over the crab body and claws.

SERVES 4

4 live cock crabs, weighing about 750g/1½lb each

Court-bouillon

1 tablespoon salt

6 whole peppercorns

2 bay leaves

½ lemon

Dressing

6 tablespoons lemon juice

2 tablespoons extra-virgin olive oil

4 tablespoons finely chopped fresh parsley

1 teaspoon finely chopped garlic

salt and freshly ground black pepper

Crab with Ginger and Soy Sauce
GRANCHI CON ZENZERO E SALSA DI SOIA

SERVES 4

4 live cock crabs, weighing about 750g/1½lb each

Court-bouillon

1 tablespoon salt

6 whole peppercorns

2 bay leaves

½ lemon

Dressing

6 tablespoons rice wine vinegar

2 tablespoons dark soy sauce

5 tablespoons finely chopped fresh ginger

1 teaspoon finely chopped garlic

2 teaspoons sugar

2 spring onions, finely chopped

8 spring onions

Bring a pan of water, large enough to hold the 4 crabs with plenty of room, to the boil. Season the water with the salt, peppercorns, bay leaves and lemon. Add the crabs—upside down so the claws will not break off—and bring the water back to the boil. Boil for 5 minutes, turn off the heat and leave the crabs in the water for 15 minutes, then plunge them into cold water, drain, and leave to get cold.

•

Remove all the white meat from the body, leaving the brown meat inside the shell. Be careful to discard the possibly poisonous dead men's fingers. These are gills which filter water, the purity of which cannot be guaranteed. Return the white meat to the body shell and crack the claw shells to expose the meat.

•

Make the dressing with the rice wine vinegar, dark soy sauce, ginger, garlic, sugar and 2 finely chopped spring onions. Mix the sauce with a fork to amalgamate well. Spoon some of the sauce over the crab body and claws. Serve with 2 spring onions per person.

SALT COD WITH WHITE WINE, TOMATO AND ROSEMARY

BACCALÀ MARCHIGIANO

First soak the baccalà for 48 hours, changing the water every 4 hours or leave it for this long under a gently running tap. In a heavy shallow pan, fry the garlic and rosemary in the oil for a few seconds, add the diced tomato and fry briefly. Stir in the tomato purée, white wine and pepper to taste. Bring the mixture to the boil, then reduce the heat and add the baccalà. Simmer gently for 15–20 minutes, depending on the thickness of the fish.

Serve with soft polenta and boiled potatoes.

•

SALT COD *Salt cod came about via the Basques, who used to catch whales in the early part of the thirteenth century. Apparently whales were very numerous in the Bay of Biscay and Bay of Gascony. The Basques used to salt and dry the whale meat, but unfortunately, probably through over-hunting, the whales became scarce so the Basques moved North to fish for cod, and proceeded to salt and dry them as they had done the whale meat. Spanish and Portuguese fishermen soon followed suit, and thus started a very flourishing industry.*

Previous to this, the Vikings had been catching cod, but instead of salting it they had only air-dried it. Air-dried cod was one of their main sources of nutrition on long sea voyages. In the seventeenth century the Norwegians started to salt cod, as their air-drying system was threatened. The Norwegians now have practically a monopoly on the salt-cod trade.

SERVES 4

4 pieces baccalà (salt cod), weighing 200g/7oz each

2 cloves garlic, finely chopped

1 sprig rosemary

6 tablespoons extra-virgin olive oil

500g/1lb 2oz plum tomatoes, peeled, seeded and diced

1 tablespoon tomato purée

1 glass dry white wine

freshly ground black pepper

In Italy, the Venetians and Genoese were the first to use salt cod, then Naples and Sicily followed, but it was rarely eaten by the noble class. Bartolomeo Scappi, cook to Pius V in 1570, mentioned baccalà in his cookery book, then there was no mention of it for two hundred years. It was always considered food for the working classes. Nowadays it is considered a delicacy.

Red Mullet Anconetana
TRIGLIE ALL'ANCONETANA

SERVES 4

4 red mullet, weighing 200g/7oz each

4 slices Parma ham, do not remove the fat

8 sage leaves, finely chopped

4 tablespoons extra-virgin olive oil

juice of 1 lemon

salt and freshly ground black pepper

4 tablespoons fresh breadcrumbs

Prepare the fish. Descale, remove the head and tail, eviscerate and cut the mullet down the back bone. Remove all bones with the help of tweezers. Wipe the fillets clean.

•

Make a sandwich of 2 fillets of mullet with Parma ham and sage in the middle. Season with salt and freshly ground black pepper.

•

Make an emulsion of the olive oil and lemon juice. Arrange the mullet in a single layer in a tray and cover with the emulsion. Leave to marinate for 2 hours.

•

Cover the fish with the breadcrumbs and bake for 15 minutes in an oven set at 180°C/350°F/gas 4. The fish should have a nice golden crust. Serve at once with the cooking liquor poured round.

Mackerel with Peas in Wine and Tomato
SGOMBRO CON PISELLI IN UMIDO

Fry the onion and garlic in olive oil until golden, add the wine and reduce down by two-thirds. Add the tomato coulis and parsley, thyme and chilli. Season with salt and freshly ground black pepper.

•

Roll up the mackerel fillets and skewer with a cocktail stick. Put the mackerel rolls in the tomato sauce, add the peas and cook gently for about 10 minutes. Remove the cocktail sticks.

•

Serve in shallow soup bowls with bruschetta (page 30) seasoned with extra-virgin olive oil, crushed garlic and a couple of turns of sea salt from the salt mill.

•

Fresh-water eel can be cooked in the same way, in this case cut the eel into cutlets.

SERVES 4

4 fresh mackerel, each weighing 450g/1lb, filleted

450g/1lb peas

1 onion, finely chopped

4 cloves garlic

600ml/1pt fresh tomato coulis (page 107)

2 tablespoons finely chopped parsley

1 small sprig thyme

a good pinch of dried chilli flakes or 1 fresh red chilli (seeded but left whole)

salt and freshly ground black pepper

1 glass white wine

olive oil

Grilled Trout with Rosemary
TROTA GRIGLIATA CON ROSMARINO

SERVES 4

4 trout, preferably from the river

2 tablespoons finely chopped parsley

1 tablespoon finely chopped rosemary

4 tablespoons white breadcrumbs, made from day-old bread

salt and freshly ground black pepper

dried chilli flakes

juice of ½ lemon

½ cup extra-virgin olive oil

lemon wedges for serving

Wash the fish and trim off the fins and remove the heads. If the trout have not come via the fishmonger, eviscerate and debone them. A fishmonger will do this for you.

•

Mix the parsley, rosemary, breadcrumbs, salt, pepper, a pinch of chilli flakes and juice of half a lemon with 3 tablespoons of the olive oil. Stuff the trout with this mixture. Oil a heavy baking tray, lay the trout on it and pour the rest of the oil over the fish. Season the skin of the trout with salt. Grill the trout for 6–8 minutes in total, turning them once and sprinkling salt on the other side as you do so. When the fish are cooked, serve them with some of the cooking olive oil poured over them and lemon wedges.

•

TO CLEAN AND DEBONE A TROUT *Cut the fins off the fish with a pair of scissors. With a sharp knife make an incision the length of the belly side of the fish. Remove the intestines and wash thoroughly inside. Now remove the gills, situated at the side of the head. Flatten the fish and cut gently down one side of the back bone, being very careful not to cut through the flesh and skin. With the point of the knife detach the back bone from the head, gently ease the bone from the flesh, slip the knife under the backbone and gently pull the bone away from the flesh, using the point of the knife, from the head to the tail. The small bones pull away with the main bone. Reshape the trout—it is now ready for stuffing.*

SALMON WITH RHUBARB AND GINGER
SALMONE CON RABARBARO E ZENZERO

First make the velouté. Cook the finely chopped shallots in the butter. Pour in the Noilly Prat and reduce to a syrupy consistency, then add the fish stock and reduce by half. Stir in the cream and bring to the boil, cook gently for 10 minutes. Sieve the mixture and keep warm.

•

Blanch the ginger in boiling water and refresh under cold water. Melt the butter, add the rhubarb with enough water to cover it, and cook for about 5 minutes or until soft. Remove the rhubarb and keep in a warm place. Reduce the rhubarb cooking liquid to almost nothing, and stir in the velouté sauce. Reheat just before serving.

•

Heat a non-stick pan, add the 4 pieces of salmon and lightly season with salt and freshly ground white pepper. Cook lightly on either side—leave it slightly pink in the middle. Put the velouté sauce on the plates, place the salmon on top, decorate with the rhubarb and ginger. Serve at once.

•

Julienne of ginger can be blanched and preserved in dry sherry for use when needed.

SERVES 4

4 escalopes salmon, weighing 200g/7oz each

8 stalks rhubarb, cut in 10cm/4in pieces

1 piece fresh ginger, 4cm/1in thick, peeled and cut into very fine julienne

20g/¾oz butter

salt and freshly ground white pepper

Velouté

5 shallots, finely chopped

15g/½oz butter

300ml/½pt Noilly Prat

300ml/½pt fish stock

300ml/½pt double cream

GRANVILLE SAUCE FOR POACHED SALMON

SERVES 2–3

1 shallot, finely chopped

4 anchovy fillets, mashed

2 tablespoons dry sherry

½ tablespoon white wine vinegar

6 whole peppercorns, cracked

pinch of ground mace

pinch of freshly grated nutmeg

30g/1oz butter

1 level tablespoon flour

6 generous tablespoons double cream

Cook the shallot, anchovy, sherry, vinegar and spices in a bain-marie until the shallot is soft. Meanwhile melt 30g/1oz butter in a small pan and add the flour. Stir in to make a roux. Cook the roux well, then add it to the shallot mixture. Mix in well and cook for a few more minutes, stirring all the time, then add the double cream. Beat it in well and cook for 2 minutes, then strain through a fine sieve.

•

This sauce is served with poached or grilled salmon.

•

Adapted from Lady Llanover's Good Cookery *published in 1867.*

Salmon and Samphire Coulis

To prepare samphire coulis, gently cook the leek and potato in a little butter until soft but not coloured. Add the chicken stock and bring to the boil, then simmer until the potato is cooked. Add the samphire. Leave for 1 minute only to keep the colour. Liquidize the ingredients and pass through a fine sieve. Add a pinch of nutmeg, a little lemon juice and pepper to taste. Samphire is naturally salty, so no need to add more salt.

●

Season the salmon lightly, cook for a minute or two on each side in a non-stick frying pan. The salmon should be just cooked through. Pour some coulis onto each plate, place an escalope on top and decorate with blanched samphire. Serve at once.

●

SAMPHIRE *We pick samphire at Crofty, near Penclawdd on the Gower coast of Wales. It grows on the salt marshes and is to be found from May to September. It is wonderfully salty and succulent and has a very definite taste of the sea. A very pleasant way of eating it, is to blanch it quickly and pour melted butter over. Eat the samphire, as you would asparagus ... with the fingers.*

SERVES 4

4 escalopes of salmon weighing 175g/6oz each

salt

Samphire coulis

1 leek finely chopped, white part only

1 medium potato, finely chopped

butter

300ml/½pt light chicken stock

225g/8oz samphire

pinch of freshly grated nutmeg

lemon juice

freshly ground white pepper

blanched samphire to decorate

CURRIED PRAWNS AND PINEAPPLE

SERVES 4

750g/1½lb live prawns

1 onion, finely chopped

1 clove garlic, finely chopped

2 tablespoons curry powder

2 plum tomatoes (or 2 very ripe tomatoes) peeled, seeded and chopped

300ml/½pt hot water

30g/1oz butter

30g/1oz flour

salt and freshly ground black pepper

2 small pineapples

3 tablespoons light olive oil or vegetable oil

chopped spring onion for garnish

Boil the live prawns in boiling salted water for 10 minutes. Drain, peel and remove the black cord. Heat 3 tablespoons of oil in a pan, add the onion, garlic and curry powder. Cook, stirring all the time, for 5 minutes or until the oil separates from the onion. Do not allow to brown. Add the tomatoes and cook for 2–3 minutes, then add the hot water and simmer for 15 minutes.

•

Blend the butter and flour and add in small pieces to the pan. Blend in well with a balloon whisk, cook for 3 minutes. Add the prawns and bring to the boil again. Season with salt and pepper. Remove from the heat.

•

Halve the pineapples, cutting them lengthways, leaving some leaves on each half. Hollow out some of the flesh and cube. Warm the pineapples and cubes in the oven or microwave. Fill the hollows with the prawn mixture, put pineapple cubes on top and sprinkle with chopped spring onion. Serve with plain boiled rice.

Monkfish and Scallops with Samphire Coulis and Fried Seaweed

SERVES 4

4 pieces monkfish, weighing 175g/6oz each

4 scallops

olive oil

2 large knobs butter

4 tablespoons fresh breadcrumbs, flavoured with grated lemon zest, chopped parsley and thyme to taste

30g/1oz seaweed, deep-fried and sprinkled with salt and chilli pepper flakes

12 sprigs samphire, blanched

a little flour

salt and freshly ground black pepper

Samphire coulis

1 leek finely chopped, white part only

1 medium potato, finely chopped

butter

300ml/½pt light chicken stock

225g/8oz samphire

pinch of freshly grated nutmeg

fresh lemon juice

freshly ground white pepper

First make the samphire coulis. Gently sweat the leek and potato in a little butter until soft; do not allow to colour. Add the chicken stock and bring to the boil, then simmer until the potato is cooked. Add the samphire, cook for 1 minute only to keep the colour. Liquidize all the ingredients and pass through a fine sieve. Add the nutmeg, a little lemon juice and pepper to taste, but no salt as samphire is naturally salty.

•

Lightly flour and season the monkfish and scallops. Heat enough olive oil to cover the base of an oven proof frying pan, large enough to take all the fish. Add a knob of butter and when it foams add the monkfish and scallops. Fry the fish until golden brown on both sides. Remove the scallops and keep warm. Cover the monkfish with the bread-crumb mixture, transfer the pan to a hot oven, 220°C/425°F/gas 7, for approximately 4–5 minutes. Be careful not to overcook, the time will depend on the thickness of the fish. The bread-crumbs will form a crust at this stage.

•

Leave the fish to rest while you prepare the plates. Put 3 tablespoons of samphire coulis on each plate, slice the monkfish pieces into 3 slices, cutting diagonally, and place the slices slightly overlapping in a half moon shape. Add the scallops. Surround wth deep-fried laver (page 46). Add a few sprigs of blanched samphire on top of the scallops. Serve immediately.

Mixed Fried Seafood (Squid and Prawns)
FRITTURA DI PESCE (SEPPIE E GAMBERI)

SERVES 4

600g/1¼lb fresh Dublin Bay prawns

600g/1¼lb small squid

flour

salt

olive oil

lemon wedges for serving

Peel the prawns and devein them. Clean the squid and cut the body into rings. Pat the seafood dry and dip them into flour seasoned with a little salt. Deep-fry the fish in hot olive oil, then drain on paper towels. Serve sprinkled with salt and lemon wedges.

•

This is another dish found everywhere on the Marche coast.

Skate with Black Olives and Caper Fruit
RAZZA CON OLIVE NERI E FRUTTI DI CAPPERI

Heat the oil in an ovenproof pan, dust the skate with flour. Brown the fish in the oil on both sides and add the garlic to the oil. Add the caper fruit, olives, oregano, lemon juice, and salt and pepper to taste, to the dish. Cover the fish and braise in an oven set at 170°C/325°F/gas 3 for 10 minutes. Lift the skate from the sauce, return the sauce to the heat and reduce until glazed. Pour the sauce over the fish. Serve the skate sprinkled with parsley.

SERVES 4

4 pieces skate, weighing 225g/8oz each

4 tablespoons extra-virgin olive oil

flour for dusting

2 cloves garlic, finely chopped

4 tablespoons caper fruit (or salted capers, well washed)

4 tablespoons black olives, pitted and thinly sliced

1 teaspoon dried oregano

4 tablespoons fresh lemon juice

salt and freshly ground black pepper to taste

1 tablespoon finely chopped fresh parsley

WARM THAI SALAD OF SCALLOPS AND FRESH BASIL

SERVES 4

8 large scallops, washed and cut in two

2 tablespoons peanut oil

2 cloves garlic, finely chopped

2 kaffir lime leaves, very finely sliced

4 tablespoons oyster sauce

1 red chilli, seeded and finely sliced

12 basil leaves (Holy basil if possible)

12 coriander leaves

3 spring onions, finely sliced

1 head crisp lettuce

Stir fry the garlic in the peanut oil, add the kaffir lime leaves, then the scallops, washed and cut in two. Stir fry, being careful not to break them. Add the chilli and 4 tablespoons of oyster sauce with 3 tablespoons of water. Reduce the sauce briskly for a few seconds.

•

Shred the lettuce, place a handful on each of 4 plates, sprinkle with the thinly sliced spring onion, and divide the basil and coriander leaves between the plates. Arrange the scallops on top and pour the sauce over.

COCKLE AND MUSSEL PIE

Prepare the cockles and mussels and steam in a large pan until the shells open. Discard any that stay closed. Scoop out the cockles and mussels and remove the flesh from the shells. Strain the liquor given out during cooking and reserve.

●

Fry the bacon in a little olive oil until lightly crisp, add the garlic, then the leek and spring onion. Cook lightly, turning the vegetables regularly. Add the thyme, parsley and pepper to taste. Stir in 300ml/½pt of the reserved cooking liquor and bring to the boil. (If there is not enough natural juice, make up the quantity with water.) Add the roux a little at a time to thicken the sauce slightly and whisk it in well with a balloon whisk. Add the cockles and mussels and bring back to the boil. Season with pepper and add salt if necessary. Remove from the heat immediately and pour the mixture onto a tray to cool quickly.

●

Preheat the oven to 200°C/400°F/gas 6. Divide the mixture between 4 small, deep pie dishes (or large ramekins) and cover each with a lid of pastry. Brush over a little egg wash, and bake in the pre-heated oven for 30 minutes or until the pastry is golden. Serve hot.

●

This is an adapted version of an old Welsh recipe.

SERVES 4

1.2 litres/2pt cockles

600 ml/1pt mussels

225g/8oz streaky bacon, diced

olive oil

1 small clove garlic, finely chopped

6 tablespoons finely sliced leek, white part only

3 tablespoons finely sliced spring onion

1 teaspoon chopped fresh thyme

2 teaspoons finely chopped parsley

salt and freshly ground black pepper

roux (a knob of butter worked with 1 tablespoon of flour)

250g/8oz prepared puff pastry

egg wash

VEGETABLES

Vegetables to the Italians mean not only a contorno*—a side dish—to go with the main meal but also a dish on their own, to be served as an antipasto, or even as a main course, if they have been prepared with a meat stuffing. In the past this was very common as it made a small amount of meat go further. Vegetables are stuffed, grilled, fried, baked, but rarely plain boiled. If a vegetable such as spinach or* cicoria *(chicory) is boiled it is then tossed in oil and garlic. Wild vegetables are very much used in the Marche as are wild salad leaves and herbs.*

Greengrocers and market stalls are piled high with locally grown vegetables, still damp from being freshly picked. Stall holders and shopkeepers will prepare vegetables for soups like minestrone, or zuppa di verdura *(vegetable soup); they will also pod peas and shell beans if requested.*

Two Italian farmers, Peppe and Pasquale, who farm locally, supply us with good organic vegetables and various salad leaves for most of the year. Franco grows his own herbs and also some of the vegetables we use, such as cardoons, celery, artichokes and many others.

It is our policy to use only local seasonal vegetables, and of course each season brings its different types. In winter parsnips are chipped and blanched and then deep-fried and sprinkled with salt. They are far tastier than potato chips. Radicchio is transformed by being dipped in egg and then breadcrumbs and deep-fried.

Spring brings purple sprouting broccoli, boiled, tossed in extra-virgin olive oil with garlic and chilli. Next come broad beans, cooked with bacon and garlic, asparagus quickly follows on. Summer brings zucchini to cook with tomato and golden zucchini flowers. In autumn there are orange pumpkins to stuff ravioli with.

Locals bring us their surplus crops, taking great pride in their offerings. Every year brings the same faces with their overflowing baskets. The man who brings the first of the runner beans, the straightest runner beans you have ever seen, comes to the back door with his basket. In thirty years he has only shyly said each year, "A few beans for you, good day."

The children from the farms around bring field mushrooms and grown-ups go searching for wild mushrooms. Excited faces peer around the back door, "Franco, look what we have found." These are the moments which tie one to a place for thirty years.

Spinach Rissoles
POLPETTINE DI SPINACI

Wash the spinach thoroughly, cook only in the water left on the leaves. Drain well, pressing between 2 plates is a quick method. Chop the spinach. Beat the eggs and add them to the Parmesan, nutmeg and breadcrumbs. Add the spinach and season with salt and freshly ground black pepper.

•

Shape into polpette (rissoles) and fry in the olive oil until golden, about 4 minutes.

SERVES 6

450g/1lb spinach

2 eggs

4 tablespoons freshly grated Parmesan cheese

¼ nutmeg, freshly grated

30g/1oz breadcrumbs from day-old bread

salt and freshly ground black pepper

6 tablespoons olive oil

Potatoes with Garlic
PATATE CROCCANTI AL BURRO D'AGLIO

Peel the potatoes and cut in slices ½cm/¼in to 1cm/½in from the base of each. Be careful not to cut through. Place the potatoes in a dish, pour over the stock and season with salt and freshly ground black pepper.

•

Mix the crushed garlic and butter together and spread between the slices and over the potatoes. Cook uncovered in an oven preheated to 180°C/350°F/gas 4 for 1 hour. The stock will be absorbed and the potatoes golden.

SERVES 4

8 potatoes, 150g/5oz each

200ml/7fl oz meat stock or vegetable stock for vegetarians

salt and freshly ground black pepper

50g/2oz butter

1 clove garlic, crushed

GRATIN OF CAULIFLOWER WITH PROSCIUTTO
CAVOLFIORE AL GRATIN CON PROSCIUTTO

SERVES 4

1 large cauliflower

Béchamel

50g/2oz butter

50g/2oz flour

600ml/1pt milk, warmed

pinch of freshly grated nutmeg

125g/4oz freshly grated Parmesan cheese

50g/2oz lean Parma ham, cut in julienne

salt and freshly ground white pepper

Melt the butter, add the flour and stir in well, add the warmed milk, slowly stirring all the time to avoid lumps. Cook for 5 minutes, still stirring, then add the nutmeg, Parmesan, Parma ham, salt and pepper, stir in well and remove from the heat.

•

Cut the cauliflower into quarters, boil in salted water until cooked, and drain. Put in a gratin dish, pour over the sauce, sprinkle with more Parmesan and cook in an oven preheated to 180°C/350°F/gas 4 for 15 minutes.

PEPPERS ABBRUZZESE
PEPERONI ABBRUZZESE

SERVES 6

18 long green peppers, or 150g/5oz peppers per person

4 cloves garlic, finely chopped

6 small red chillies, seeded and finely chopped (less can be used)

1½ tablespoons dried oregano

salt and freshly ground black pepper

4 tablespoons extra-virgin olive oil

Wash the peppers and cut them in half lengthwise. Remove the seeds and white veins. Scatter the finely chopped garlic and seeded chilli in the hollows of the peppers. Sprinkle over the dried oregano, and season with salt and pepper. Dribble over the olive oil and bake in a preheated oven 180°C/350°F/gas 4 for 10–12 minutes. Serve hot or at room temperature.

Grilled Stuffed Mushrooms

FUNGHI FARCITI ALLA GRIGLIA

SERVES 4

8 large wild field mushrooms, or large cultivated ones

3 cloves garlic, finely chopped

3 tablespoons parsley, finely chopped

1 teaspoon fresh red chilli, finely chopped (less chilli can be used)

salt and freshly ground black pepper

6 tablespoons fresh breadcrumbs

60ml/2fl oz extra-virgin olive oil

Remove the stalks from the mushrooms and wipe the mushrooms with a damp cloth. Mix the garlic, parsley, chilli, salt and pepper into the breadcrumbs. Use the mixture to fill the mushroom cups, dividing it evenly. Dribble the extra-virgin olive oil over the mushrooms, then grill for 10 minutes. Serve hot.

Zucchini "Chips"

"CHIPS" DI ZUCCHINI FRITTI

SERVES 6

1kg/2½lb zucchini

salt

flour

light olive oil for deep frying

roasted Schezuan pepper and salt (page 46)

Cut the zucchini into matchstick chips (do not peel the zucchini). Put the chips in a colander, sprinkle with salt and leave to drain for 1 hour. Wash and dry the zucchini chips thoroughly. Now dip the chips in flour, shake off the excess, and deep-fry in hot light olive oil until golden and crisp. Remove the chips from the oil with a perforated spoon and drain on absorbent paper. Sprinkle with ground roasted Schezuan pepper (page 46) and salt. Serve at once.

ZUCCHINI TOPS
CIME DI ZUCCHINI

SERVES 4

550g/1¼lb zucchini tops

4 tablespoons extra-virgin olive oil

2 cloves garlic, finely chopped

coarse sea salt and freshly ground black pepper

4 slices bruschetta or polenta (page 99)

When the zucchini plants have finished flowering you are left with little clusters of tiny zucchini and tender leaves sprouting from the top. Before you pull the plants up, nip these tops off; the clusters should be cut about 8–10cm/3–4in long. It is a tradition in the Marche to serve these cime di zucchini *with bruschetta or* polenta alla marchigiana *(page 103) as a first course or as a* contorno, *a side vegetable dish. In the early part of the autumn women from the farms bring bunches of these cime to sell in the markets. Everyone loves these final offerings of the summer season.*

•

Steam the zucchini tops for about 10 minutes. Heat 4 tablespoons of olive oil in a frying pan and add the finely chopped garlic, fry briefly, add the zucchini tops and fry them, being careful not to break them up. Season with coarse sea salt and freshly ground black pepper. Serve on bruschetta or grilled polenta, with a wedge of lemon.

Fried Radicchio
FRITTURA DI RADICCHIO

SERVES 4

1 large head radicchio

flour

2 beaten eggs, seasoned with salt and freshly ground black pepper

dry breadcrumbs

lemon

Remove the outer leaves from the radicchio. Wash and thoroughly dry the radicchio and cut it into four. Dust the quarters with flour, separating the leaves as you do so. Now dip them into the beaten eggs, keeping the leaves as separate as possible. Then dust lightly with breadcrumbs. Deep fry the radicchio quarters and then drain them on absorbent kitchen paper to remove any surplus oil. Season with salt and serve at once with a wedge of lemon. The finished result should look like a flower.

Grilled Radicchio with Parmesan and Truffles
RADICCHIO TREVISANO ALLA GRIGLIA

SERVES 4

4 small or 2 large heads radicchio di Treviso

3 tablespoons extra-virgin olive oil

salt and freshly ground black pepper

115g/4oz Parmesan cheese, cut in fine slivers

2 white truffles, shaved

Remove any damaged leaves from the radicchio heads, cut each in half, or in quarters depending on the size, and wash thoroughly. Leave to drain in a colander.

•

Put the radicchio on a large plate and dribble the olive oil over the top. Season well with salt and freshly ground black pepper. Heat a large frying pan and, when hot, add the radicchio pieces in one layer only. Cover the pan, reduce the flame to moderate and cook for 2–3 minutes, turning the radicchio pieces once. Arrange the Parmesan slivers on top of the radicchio and flash under a hot grill until the cheese has melted. Top with the shaved truffle and serve at once.

•

If you would prefer a crisper version of this dish, put the radicchio in a hot frying pan over a high heat and leave uncovered, turning once during the cooking time.

AUBERGINES CALABRESE
MELANZANE ALLA CALABRESE

SERVES 4

2 aubergines, weighing approx. 450g/1lb each

coarse salt

6 plum tomatoes or ripe ordinary tomatoes, peeled, seeded and diced

2 cloves garlic

2 tablespoons light olive oil

2 red chilli peppers, seeded and sliced thinly

1 sprig parsley, chopped

6 mint leaves, chopped

freshly ground black pepper

Good as a first course or as a vegetable with simply cooked meat.

•

Wash the aubergines and slice lengthwise, about 1cm/½in thick. Sprinkle the slices with salt and leave in a colander to drain for 1 hour. Dry the slices well and place them on a preheated ridged griddle and cook until lightly brown on either side, turning once during cooking only.

•

Arrange the slices on a serving dish and keep warm. Finely chop the garlic and fry briefly in the olive oil. Add the diced tomatoes and sauté briefly; they must keep their dice shape. Add the chilli and herbs, season with salt and pepper.

•

Spoon the tomato mixture on top of the aubergine slices. Serve either hot or at room temperature.

MILANESE AUBERGINE
MELANZANE MILANESE

Slice the aubergine lengthways into eight slices—about ½cm/¼in thick. Season the slices lightly with salt and lightly flour them. Then dip them into the beaten egg.

•

Fry the slices in foaming oil and butter. When they are golden on both sides, drain them on absorbent paper, sprinkle with salt and serve at once. These slices must be hot and crisp.

•

Aubergine slices are good as part of a vegetarian dish. They can also be dipped in egg and dry breadcrumbs and fried.

SERVES 4

1 medium purple aubergine

2 eggs, beaten

a little flour

125ml/4fl oz olive oil

butter

salt

POTATO CROCCHETTE WITH MOZZARELLA
CROCCHETTE DI PATATE CON MOZZARELLA

Cook the potatoes in a microwave, or boil, and as soon as it is possible to handle them, peel them and pass them through a mouli-légume. Add the butter and amalgamate well, then the 4 egg yolks and stir them in thoroughly. Season with salt, freshly ground pepper and mace.

•

Break off 14 pieces of the potato mixture, each about the size of a large egg. Cut the mozzarella into 14 pieces, and mould the potato round the mozzarella to give an egg shape. Roll the potatoes in flour.

•

MAKES 14 CROCCHETTE

1kg/2¼lb potatoes, unpeeled

60g/2oz butter

4 egg yolks

2 whole eggs

a little freshly ground mace

salt and freshly ground black pepper

(continued overleaf)

3 mozzarella, about 290g/10oz in total

flour

dry breadcrumbs

freshly grated Parmesan cheese (optional)

light olive oil for frying

Beat 2 eggs with a little salt. Dip the potatoes in the egg and then in the breadcrumbs (a little Parmesan cheese can be added to the breadcrumbs). Deep-fry the potato crocchette in light olive oil until they are golden. Drain on absorbent kitchen paper.

Purée of Potato and Leek with Caerphilly Cheese

SERVES 4

450g/1lb potatoes

175g/6oz leeks, finely sliced

60g/2oz butter

½ cup warm milk

salt and freshly ground white pepper

2 pinches freshly grated nutmeg

Caerphilly cheese, grated

These potatoes go well with lamb.

•

Boil and drain the potatoes and pass through the mouli-légume.

•

Gently cook the leeks in the butter until softened; be careful not to allow them to colour. Purée the leeks in a blender. Mix together the potatoes, leek, butter, milk, salt, pepper and nutmeg. Put the mixture in a buttered gratin dish and sprinkle grated Caerphilly cheese on top. Bake the potato and leek gratin in an oven set at 200°C/400°F/gas 6 until the cheese is bubbling and golden.

Potato and Cep Gallette
GALLETTE DI PATATE E PORCINI

Boil the potatoes in their skins, drain, peel them and pass them through a vegetable mill. Add the butter, Parmesan cheese, egg yolks, salt, freshly ground black pepper and the finely chopped parsley. Fold in well with the potato. Chop the mushrooms into small dice, fry them in olive oil, season with salt and pepper, and fold them into the potato mixture. The texture of the mixture should be dry. Flour a pastry board and roll the potato 1cm/½in thick, then cut it into 7.5cm/3in circles. Gently dust them with more flour. Fry the potato cakes in a little foaming butter and olive oil until they are golden brown. Dry them on absorbent kitchen paper and serve at once.

SERVES 4

400g/14oz potatoes

100g/3½oz porcini, or chestnut mushrooms and shitake mixed

20g/¾oz butter

2 egg yolks

15g/½oz freshly grated Parmesan cheese

2 tablespoons finely chopped parsley

plain flour

1 tablespoon extra-virgin olive oil

salt and freshly ground black pepper

butter and olive oil for frying

BAKED FENNEL WITH PARSLEY AND BREADCRUMBS

FINOCCHI ALLA GIUDEA

SERVES 4

4 fennel bulbs

60g/2oz fresh white breadcrumbs

1 clove garlic, finely chopped

1 tablespoon finely chopped parsley

salt and freshly ground black pepper

3 tablespoons extra-virgin olive oil

Cut the fennel bulbs in half and remove the tough outer leaves. Blanch the pieces in boiling water for 10 minutes and drain well.

•

Mix together the fresh breadcrumbs, garlic, parsley, salt and freshly ground black pepper. Open the fennel leaves and stuff the breadcrumb mixture between the leaves. Place the fennel in a gratin dish, pour the olive oil over the fennel and bake in an oven set at 180°C/350°F/gas 4 for 12 minutes, or until the breadcrumbs are golden.

ASPARAGUS BUNDLES

FAGOTTINI DI ASPARAGI

SERVES 4

900g/2lb asparagus

salt and freshly ground black pepper

slices of Parma ham

freshly grated Parmesan cheese

butter

Steam the asparagus until al dente. Divide stalks into bundles of 3 and season with salt and pepper. Wrap each bundle in a slice of Parma ham.

•

Butter a gratin dish and place the bundles in a single layer. Sprinkle freshly grated Parmesan on top and dot with little knobs of butter. Bake in a moderate oven 180°C/350°F/gas 4 for about 20 minutes. These asparagus bundles can be served as a hot first course or as a vegetable.

BREADCRUMBED ASPARAGUS
ASPARAGI PANATI

Wash and trim the asparagus. Boil in salted water for about 15 minutes or until a sharp fork penetrates the flesh easily. Be careful, the cooking time could be less. Cooking times vary, depending on the thickness, variety and age of the asparagus. The asparagus can also be steamed, which is preferable. Drain the asparagus on linen cloths.

•

Mix together the breadcrumbs and Parmesan. Dip each piece of asparagus in egg and then in the breadcrumbs and Parmesan. Leave the hardish bit of the asparagus at the base undipped. Repeat the process; each asparagus *must* be dipped twice.

•

Divide the oil and butter between 2 frying pans and heat. When foaming, fry the asparagus until they are golden. Drain on absorbent kitchen paper. Serve hot with wedges of lemon, either as part of a vegetarian fritto misto or as a vegetable on their own.

SERVES 6

1.6kg/3½lb asparagus

4 eggs, lightly beaten

200g/7oz dry breadcrumbs

100g/3½oz freshly grated Parmesan cheese

4 tablespoons olive oil

100g/3½oz butter

lemon wedges for serving

FRIED ARTICHOKES JEWISH-STYLE
CARCIOFI "ALLA GIUDEA"

SERVES 4

8 artichokes (very young ones)

olive oil

juice of ½ lemon

salt

This recipe calls for very young artichokes. The choke is left in as it will not yet have developed into fibrous matter. These artichokes, when cooked, look like bronze chrysanthemums. Carciofi alla Giudea is another Roman speciality found at Piperno Restaurant in the Jewish quarter of Rome. These artichokes are usually served as a first course; 2 per person is a recommended portion.

•

Trim the artichokes of the hard outside leaves, cut off the stalk and cut off the tips of the leaves with a sharp knife.

•

Press each artichoke down on a board so that they spread out a little. As you prepare them, drop them into a bowl of cold water with the juice of half a lemon. Drain and dry the artichokes thoroughly before frying.

•

Have ready a pan of very hot light olive oil, then plunge the artichokes in, base upwards. Turn the artichokes with tongs, making sure the leaves stay spread out.

•

Drain the artichokes, when cooked and crisp, on absorbent kitchen paper. Sprinkle with salt and serve at once.

Lentils in Wine and Tomato
LENTICCHIE IN UMIDO

Leave the lentils to soak in cold water overnight. Drain and wash them thoroughly and check for stones.

•

In a heavy pan, fry the onion, carrot and bacon in the oil until the onion is golden, add the lentils and mix into the onion mixture. Stir for a few minutes. Pour in the wine, fresh tomato coulis and enough stock just to cover the lentils. Season with salt and pepper—be generous with the pepper—and add the sage leaves. Reduce the heat, cover the pan and gently simmer the lentils, stirring occasionally. If the liquid starts to reduce too rapidly and the lentils are not yet cooked, add more stock. The final result should be a not too dry, but certainly not sloppy, texture. The lentils are used as an accompaniment for roast game, cooked either on the spit or in the oven.

SERVES 4

300g/10oz lentils (Puy or Cavellucchi)

1 small onion, finely chopped

1 medium carrot, finely chopped

2 slices bacon, finely chopped

2 tablespoons extra-virgin olive oil

1 glass dry white wine

175ml/6fl oz fresh tomato coulis (page 107)

175ml/6fl oz chicken stock

salt and freshly ground black pepper

1 sprig sage

Orange and Olive Salad
INSALATA DI ARANCE E OLIVE

SERVES 6

8 large oranges

20 pitted black olives

2 small red onions

extra-virgin olive oil

salt and freshly ground black pepper

a pinch of dried chilli flakes

small bunch of parsley, finely chopped

fresh lemon juice (optional)

Peel the oranges, making sure all the pith is removed. Segment them and divide between 6 small plates. Slice the red onions very thinly and scatter on top. Season with salt, freshly ground black pepper and chilli flakes.

•

Dress with a little extra-virgin olive oil, olives and lemon juice to taste. Sprinkle with the chopped parsley.

•

This salad is good served with plain roast meats, chicken, rabbit, etc., or even better served with chicken or turkey breasts marsala (page 145).

Leeks with Parma Ham
PORRI CON PROSCIUTTO DI PARMA

Peel and trim the leeks, removing most of the green part of the leaves. Cut the leeks into 7.5/3in lengths and then into julienne. Wash thoroughly. Leeks tend to hold soil so do wash them very carefully.

•

Slice and sweat the shallots in the olive oil and butter. Add the leeks and cook until softened. Stir in the Parma ham and season to taste. Cook briefly.

•

Serve in a small mound on each plate. This combination goes particularly well with grilled lamb dishes.

SERVES 4

6 leeks

3 shallots

1 tablespoon olive oil

15g/½oz butter

60g/2oz Parma ham, cut in julienne

salt and freshly ground black pepper

Leeks with Parma Ham
PORRI CON PROSCIUTTO DI PARMA

Peel and trim the leeks, removing most of the green part of the leaves. Cut the leeks into 7.5/3in lengths and then into julienne. Wash thoroughly. Leeks tend to hold soil so do wash them very carefully.

•

Slice and sweat the shallots in the olive oil and butter. Add the leeks and cook until softened. Stir in the Parma ham and season to taste. Cook briefly.

•

Serve in a small mound on each plate. This combination goes particularly well with grilled lamb dishes.

SERVES 4

6 leeks

3 shallots

1 tablespoon olive oil

15g/½oz butter

60g/2oz Parma ham, cut in julienne

salt and freshly ground black pepper

SWEETS

Every town in Italy has a good pasticceria or two. Italians love eating sweet foods, although generally speaking Italian housewives do not make their own gateaux, preferring to leave the expert to make them.

Sweets are not eaten every day in an Italian household but reserved for special occasions, national holidays and feast days, of which there seem to be so many, so there is always an excuse to buy special cakes! Fruit is served after a meal on ordinary days. On Mother's Day in Italy, children and adults buy wonderful pastry creations to deliver to their mothers and grandmothers. With their arms laden with flowers and beribboned boxes of cakes they are a sight to see.

My (Ann's) mother has been the main source of inspiration for our cakes. The recipe for the very popular torte *with three liqueurs was given to her years ago by Franco's Aunt Mema. This aunt loved sweets, whereas my mother rarely eats them, but just likes making them, which is rather fortunate. Anna, who hails from Southern Italy, where ice creams are renowned, is the ice cream and sorbet maker. Anna has a reputation for making everything she sees into ice cream. Too bad if one had another idea for some fruit—in a flash it's churning away in the ice-cream machine.*

We are fortunate that we have very good fruit farms near us. The fruit for the ice creams is picked first thing in the morning and made into ices by lunch time. Children come with baskets of wild berries, such as blackberries and whimberries. Franco encourages them to tell their friends to go picking as well. Sometimes we are swamped with wild berries.

Simple home-made sweets such as sfrappe *and* castagnole *(a type of doughnut) are made for carnival. Cakes and sweets made at home usually have a tradition behind them. In the country special cakes were made to celebrate the end of reaping or threshing or the grape harvest. In the Marche this tradition still carries on. This was the custom in Wales as well but seems to be dying out here.*

Many of the cakes and sweets made by the Marchigiana housewife also have a lot of folklore behind them. One year when I was in Italy with my mother, some local women came to ask us if they could use our outside oven to bake a soft macaroon sweet called serpe *(serpent). It is considered to taste better if cooked in a wood-fired oven. At Christmas, the eating of the serpent is almost a rite, symbolizing the death of original sin brought about by the birth of the infant Christ.*

Zuppa Inglese

I (Ann) read this explanation of zuppa inglese *in* The Daily Telegraph *a few years ago: "The story goes that sailors from Nelson's ships went ashore at Naples with bottles of rum. At the close of a good meal they wanted a pudding instead of the fruit usually provided after meals. A sponge cake was produced, over which they poured the rum. The fruit was then cut up and put on top. Over all this was poured a substance called zabaione which is a cream-like liquid made with eggs, sugar and Marsala. This was eaten with great relish by the British and later by the Italians, who called it* zuppa inglese."

•

Halve and poach the apricots in a little syrup, drain and leave to cool. To make the custard, whisk the egg yolks in the top of a bain-marie. Add the sugar and whisk till the eggs and sugar are creamy. Whisk in the sieved flour, making sure there are no lumps. Add the milk a little at a time, always whisking, then the vanilla pod and lemon peel. Place the top of the bain-marie on the bain-marie base; the water in the base should be only gently rippling. Whisk the egg mixture until it thickens. Remove the pan from the heat and leave the custard to cool. Before using the custard, remove the vanilla pod and lemon peel.

•

Cut the pan di spagna into 1cm/½in slices. Divide the slices between 2 trays and sprinkle Alchermes or Marsala on one half and rum on the other half. The sponge must be evenly soaked but not soggy.

•

SERVES 4

200g/7oz pan di spagna (page 231)

Alchermes (page 226) or Marsala

rum

175g/6oz fresh apricots

a little syrup

Confectioner's custard

3 egg yolks

90g/3oz caster sugar

40g/1½oz flour, sieved

½ litre/¾pt warm milk

½ vanilla pod

1 slice lemon peel, without the pith

½ litre/1pt whipped cream

Layer the slices of sponge alternately, putting a layer of custard between each one. Place the zuppa in the refrigerator until ready to serve. Before serving, spread the whipped cream over the top and sides, and decorate the top with the drained poached apricots.

•

ALCHERMES *A beautiful crimson coloured liqueur. It gets its colour from cochineal. It is made with spices—cinnamon, cloves, nutmeg, mace and coriander and also jasmin and iris. Alchermes is always used in sweets, for example, zuppa inglese, or splashed on* stracci *(doughnuts), and stuffed sweet deep-fried courgette flowers.*

If you cannot obtain Alchermes do not look for a substitute, use sweet Marsala instead. The colour will not be so effective but the taste will be good.

Bavarois of Raspberries

Sieve the raspberries into a bowl and add the lemon juice and sugar.

•

Dissolve the gelatine in a bain-marie with a little of the raspberry juice. Pour the milk into a blender, add the gelatine mixture and blend for 1 minute. Add the raspberry purée, lemon and sugar mixture, then the egg yolks. Blend for 5 seconds. Remove the cover, add the cream and crushed ice, and keep blending until smooth. Pour into individual bavarois moulds and place in the fridge. When set, tip out of the moulds and serve with a raspberry coulis (below) and surround with a few frosted raspberries. To frost raspberries simply roll them in caster sugar.

SERVES 4–6

750g/1½lb raspberries

juice of 1 lemon

8 tablespoons sugar

1½ level tablespoons gelatine powder

4 tablespoons milk

2 egg yolks

300ml/½pt double cream

1 cup crushed ice

Raspberry Coulis

Mix all the ingredients together. Add less sugar if the raspberries are very sweet.

SERVES 4–6

250g/½lb sieved raspberries

2 tablespoons Kirsch

3 tablespoons caster sugar

juice of ½ lemon

OMELETTE SOUFFLÉ AU GRAND MARNIER

SERVES 2

3 eggs

2 tablespoons sugar

1 sherry glass Grand Marnier

nut of butter

Separate the eggs. Add the sugar and Grand Marnier to the yolks and whisk briefly. Whisk the egg whites until stiff. Fold egg whites into yolk mixture.

•

Heat two 15cm/6in omelette pans. Put a small nut of butter in the pans. When melted, quickly pour in the egg mixture, giving the pan a shake. When the base of the soufflé omelette is lightly browned, using a spatula, flip half the omelette over the other half, tipping onto a warm plate at the same time. Warmed strawberries can be placed on one half before folding.

•

Sprinkle with sugar and make criss-cross patterns on the top with a previously heated very hot poker. Serve at once.

•

This last process can be omitted if you feel you cannot do it quickly enough. Speed is very important or the soufflé will collapse.

ZABAGLIONE

SERVES 4

4 egg yolks

4 tablespoons sugar

8 tablespoons Marsala

amaretti biscuits

Put all the ingredients in the top of a bain-marie. Whisk the mixture with a balloon whisk. It will be frothy first of all, but will eventually thicken. When the mixture starts to come away from the sides of the pan, it is ready. Pour the mixture into tall wine glasses and serve with amaretti biscuits.

Spumoni Amaretto

Whisk the yolks with sugar until creamy. Add the amaretto liqueur slowly and continue whisking to bind the mixture. Fold in the whisked cream. Pour into dessert glasses and freeze. Serve with crumbled amaretti biscuits on the top.

SERVES 10

9 egg yolks

8 tablespoons sugar

1 wine glass amaretto liqueur

300ml/½pt double cream, whisked to thicken slightly

amaretti biscuits

Bavarian Pudding

Hard boil the eggs for 10 minutes. Plunge into cold water, peel and retain only the yolk.

•

Beat the butter and sugar until creamy. Pass the egg yolks through a fine sieve, add them to the butter and sugar, and beat well until light and fluffy. Stir in the walnuts. Divide the mixture into two.

•

Divide the biscuits into four layers. Line an oblong tin (18×9×5cm/7×3½×2in) with clingfilm. Dip one layer of biscuits in the rum, and put a layer of cream mixture on the top. Dip a second layer of biscuits in cherry brandy and put on top of the cream, then dip the third layer in the remaining rum and cover with cream. Finish with a layer of biscuits dipped in cherry brandy. Sprinkle caster sugar on top. Leave in the fridge for 24 hours before using.

SERVES 6

3 eggs

60g/2oz butter

90g/3oz caster sugar

60g/2oz walnuts, roughly chopped

150ml/¼pt rum

150ml/¼pt cherry brandy

24 boudoir biscuits

Sicilian Cheesecake

CASSATA SICILIANA

1 pan di spagna (page 231), sliced into 4 slabs

450g/1lb ricotta

30g/1oz sugar

2 tablespoons double cream

4 heaped tablespoons chopped mixed candied fruit peel

60g/2oz plain chocolate, coarsely chopped

Strega or Maraschino

Coating

225g/8oz plain or bitter chocolate

6 tablespoons espresso coffee

175g/6oz butter

Pass the ricotta through a food mill, add the sugar and cream, and beat until smooth. Fold in the candied peel and chopped chocolate.

•

Sprinkle the bottom slab of sponge with liqueur, cover generously with the ricotta mixture, and place another slab of sponge cake on top. Repeat this process with Strega and ricotta until all the slabs are used up. End with a plain slice of sponge cake. Gently press the loaf together to make it compact and refrigerate for at least 2 hours.

•

To make the coating, melt the dark chocolate with the espresso coffee in a bain-marie over a low heat. Beat in the butter, a knob at a time. Beat until thickened to a spreading consistency. Spread the chocolate all over the sponge cake. Refrigerate for at least a day before using.

Plain Sponge Cake

PAN DI SPAGNA

Preheat the oven to 180°C/350°F/gas 4. Grease a swiss roll tin (22½ × 7½ × 7½cm/9 × 3 × 3in) and line it with greased greaseproof paper.

•

Separate the eggs, add the sugar to the yolks and whisk until the mixture is fluffy. With a clean dry whisk, whisk the whites until stiff. Fold the egg whites with a metal spoon into the egg and sugar mixture, alternating with the sifted flour and baking powder. Spoon the mixture into the prepared tin and bake for 10 minutes. Leave the cake in the tin for 5 minutes before turning out onto a wire rack. When cool, slice into 4 equal pieces.

2 eggs, size 3

45g/1½oz caster sugar

45g/1½oz plain flour, sifted

¼ teaspoon baking powder

Touraine Chestnut Pudding

Make this pudding a day in advance. Cream together the butter and icing sugar, then add the melted chocolate and beat well. Push the chestnut purée through a fine sieve, then add a little at a time to the creamed mixture, alternating with a little brandy until well amalgamated and all the purée and brandy have been incorporated.

•

Transfer the mixture to an 18×9×5cm/7×3½×2in rectangular dish. Smooth the surface to make it level and refrigerate for 24 hours. Turn out, slice and decorate with strawberries and fresh cream or crème anglaise.

SERVES 6

100g/3½oz unsalted butter

100g/3½oz icing sugar, sifted

125g/4½oz plain chocolate, melted

1 can (425g/15oz) natural chestnut purée

good quality brandy

strawberries and cream to decorate

Dolce Torinese

SERVES 6–8

225g/8oz plain or bitter chocolate

125ml/4fl oz dark rum

225g/8oz unsalted butter

60g/2oz icing sugar, sifted

2 egg yolks

150g/5oz finely chopped blanched almonds

12 petit beurre biscuits

fresh cream for serving

Cream the butter until very pale and fluffy. Beat in the icing sugar. Add the egg yolks one at a time, whipping steadily. Soften the chocolate over hot water, beat well, add the rum, then leave to cool a little.

•

Add the almonds to the butter mixture, then add the chocolate mixture. Fold in the biscuits, chopped into small pieces. Pour the mixture into a buttered tin, about 21×10×6cm/8½×4×2½in, and chill. To serve, unmould and cut into slices, and serve with fresh cream on top.

Malakoff Torte

SERVES 6

175g/6oz butter

175g/6oz caster sugar

1 egg yolk

90g/3oz plain or bitter chocolate, melted

2 tablespoons dark rum

20–30 sponge finger biscuits

Mix the butter, sugar, egg yolk and melted chocolate to a smooth cream.

•

Almost fill a cup with cold water, add the rum and pour into a bowl. Dip the biscuits in the liquid, but do not saturate them. Place a layer of sponge fingers in an oblong tin (21×10×6cm/8½×4×2½in) lined with greaseproof paper. Follow this by a layer of the cream mixture. Continue to fill the tin alternately layering with sponge fingers and cream mixture until all is used up, ending with sponge biscuits. Place a lid on the tin and a weight on the top to hold it down. Refrigerate for 2–3 hours, before serving.

Queen Charlotte's Tart

Sieve flour and sugar into a bowl, rub in the butter until mixture resembles breadcrumbs. Use your hands lightly. Beat the egg and add chilled water, sprinkle over dough and work in lightly with your fingertips. Leave the dough in a refrigerator for half an hour.

•

Grate all the peel from the oranges and lemon. Squeeze the juice from the oranges and lemon, mix with the grated peel. Beat the egg yolks with 120g/4oz of the sugar until creamy and add to the juice and peel.

•

Line a round baking tin with the pastry and pour in the mixture. Bake for 40 minutes at 160°C/300°F/gas 2. Meanwhile, beat the egg whites with the remaining sugar till they hold a peak. Quickly pile on top of the hot tart and return to the oven for 10 minutes. The meringue should be biscuit coloured and crisp on top but soft inside. Serve hot.

•

This is an adaptation from a recipe from Lady Llanover's First Principles of Good Cookery, *1867.*

SERVES 6

Pastry

175g/6oz flour

90g/3oz butter

½ tablespoon caster sugar

1 egg yolk

a little water

Topping

2 oranges

1 lemon

150g/5oz sugar

5 eggs, yolks and whites separated

GÂTEAU AMBASSADEUR

SERVES 8

90g/3oz black grapes, pips removed

60ml/2fl oz brandy

100g/3½oz unsalted butter

100g/3½oz icing sugar, sifted

2 eggs, separated

115g/4oz plain or bitter chocolate

3 tablespoons double cream, whipped

100g/3½oz crumbled petit beurre biscuits

double cream to serve

Chocolate coating

115g/4oz bitter chocolate

115g/4oz unsalted butter

1 teaspoon rose-water

Soak the grapes in brandy for an hour or so. Melt the chocolate in a bain-marie.

•

Beat the butter and sugar together until light and creamy, then add the egg yolks and the melted chocolate, beating in well. Stir in the whipped cream, then the grapes, brandy and biscuits. Whip the egg whites until stiff and fold them into the mixture, carefully amalgamating all together. Line a 19cm/7½in sponge cake tin with clingfilm. Put in the mixture, smoothing the surface, then refrigerate overnight.

•

To prepare the chocolate coating, melt the chocolate in a bain-marie and mix in the butter and rosewater. When the coating is cool enough for spreading, take the cake still in its tin, and coat the exposed surface. Return the cake to the refrigerator. When the coating has set firm, take the cake out of the fridge and turn it out onto a rotary cake table. Coat the top and sides with the remaining chocolate and return it to the fridge. Serve with fresh double cream.

TORTE WITH THREE LIQUEURS
TORTA CON TRE LIQUORI

Beat the butter and sugar together until creamy. Beat the egg yolks until pale, add the egg yolks to the butter mixture and continue beating until the mixture is creamy. Add the coffee slowly to this mixture, beating until all the coffee has been amalgamated. Divide the mixture into three.

•

On a flat tray, put a layer of 7 boudoir biscuits, dipped in brandy. Cover with one-third of the cream mixture. Sprinkle with one-third of the chopped chocolate and flaked almonds. Dip the amaretti biscuits in rum and place on top of the cream and nut layer. Put the second layer of cream mixture, sprinkle with half the remaining chocolate and nuts and top with the remaining 7 biscuits dipped in Tia Maria.

•

Cover the top and sides with the last portion of cream. Scatter the remaining chocolate and nuts on the top and chill for 48 hours before serving.

SERVES 4

125g/4$\frac{1}{2}$oz butter

115g/4oz sugar

2 egg yolks

90ml/3fl oz strong black coffee

14 boudoir biscuits

30ml/1fl oz brandy

75g/2$\frac{1}{2}$oz plain or bitter chocolate, chopped into small pieces

75g/2$\frac{1}{2}$oz flaked almonds, toasted

12 amaretti biscuit halves

30ml/1fl oz rum

30ml/1fl oz Tia Maria

Pomegranate Sorbet

MAKES 1.2 LITRES/2PT

600ml/1pt fresh pomegranate juice (if the pomegranates are good juicy ones, 4 will yield a pint)

300ml/½pt red wine

juice of 1 orange

175g/6oz sugar

125ml/4fl oz water

Use a centrifugal juice and vegetable extractor to juice the pomegranates, or sieve the seeds. Make a thick syrup from the sugar and water. When cold add the pomegranate juice, wine and orange juice.

Churn the mixture in an ice-cream machine.

•

Elizabeth David sent us this recipe; she said the idea came from a book written by Gilliers who was a confectioner to Stanislas, King of Poland and father-in-law of Louis XV. The colour of this unusual sorbet is a very rich deep garnet and the flavour fine and rich.

Strawberry Water Ice

GRANITA DI FRAGOLE

SERVES 6

250g/8oz sugar

150ml/¼pt water

1kg/2¼lbs very ripe, freshly picked strawberries

juice of ½ lemon

juice of ½ orange

whole strawberries for serving

Make a syrup by boiling the sugar and water together for 5 minutes. Allow it to cool.

•

Pass the strawberries through a sieve, add the lemon and orange juice and the cooled syrup. Freeze in a sorbetière. Serve the granita with a few fresh berries dipped in caster sugar.

Persimmon Sorbet
GRANITA DI CACHI

Peel and discard the skin of the persimmons, turn the pulp into a blender and purée until smooth. There should be 600ml/1pt of purée.

•

Boil the sugar and water for about 5 minutes, to make a thin syrup. Leave the syrup to get cold, then combine it with the purée. Add the strained orange juice. Pour in the double cream and whirl once more in the blender. Churn in an ice-cream maker.

•

Elizabeth David, who gave us this recipe when we had a glut of ripe persimmons, remarked that it was a particularly delicious and pretty sorbet.

MAKES ABOUT 750ML/1¼PT

5 very ripe persimmons

115g/4oz sugar

150ml/¼pt water

juice of ½ small sweet orange, strained

150ml/¼pt double cream

Persimmons and Grappa
CACHI CON GRAPPA

There are two ways of preparing this very simple refreshing sweet, but never attempt to serve persimmons unless the fruit is very ripe, so ripe that it will split easily.

•

These beautiful orange fruit with an exquisite calyx freeze well and make a natural "sorbet". Ten minutes before serving them, remove them from the deep-freeze then slice them in half and serve with grappa poured over. They can also be eaten fresh, cut in half with the grappa poured over.

SERVES 4

4 persimmons

4 spirit measures of grappa

WHIMBERRY (BILBERRY) SORBET I

SERVES 4–6

115g/4oz sugar

150ml/¼pt water

450g/1lb bilberries (whimberries)

juice of ½ lemon

double cream or vodka, and fresh whimberries, for serving

In Wales, bilberries are known as whimberries. They grow in profusion on the Black Mountains and other surrounding mountains around Abergavenny. They are a wonderfully flavoured tiny purple fruit, with a grey bloom, which grow on low dense bushes. Back-breaking to pick but worth every effort.

•

Make a syrup by boiling the sugar and water together for 5 minutes. Allow to cool.

•

Sieve the raw berries and add the cooled syrup and lemon juice. Pour the mixture into an ice-cream machine and churn for 5 minutes. Serve with fresh double cream or pour a little vodka over the sorbet and decorate with fresh bilberries (whimberries) and sugared mint leaves.

•

SUGARED MINT LEAVES *Wash and dry the mint leaves thoroughly and paint them with a little lightly beaten egg white. Dip in caster sugar, shake off the surplus and leave to dry in the sun or in a warm place, like the airing cupboard.*

Bilberry Sorbet II

SERVES 4–6

450g/1lb bilberries

icing sugar

lemon juice

vodka

double cream for serving

Cook the berries lightly in a little water. Liquidize them, then sieve them into a bowl. Add icing sugar and lemon juice to taste, plus a half measure of vodka. Stir in well. Churn in an electric ice-cream machine.

•

Serve with a little extra vodka poured on top and a little fresh double cream.

Fig Ice Cream
GELATO DI FICHI

SERVES 6

450g/1lb fresh figs

150g/5oz sugar

200ml/7fl oz milk

juice of ½ lemon

3 tablespoons brandy

1 fresh fig per serving

Peel the figs (if you leave the skin on half the figs a speckled effect is obtained in the ice cream). Put all the figs in the food processor and blend until a creamy texture is obtained. Add the sugar, milk, lemon juice and brandy, and process a few times more. Churn in an ice-cream maker.

•

Serve the fig ice cream with a petalled fig (page 247).

ROSE PETAL ICE CREAM

MAKES 600ML/1PT

8 egg yolks

175g/6oz caster sugar

450ml/¾pt milk

3 highly perfumed large red roses, not sprayed with insecticides

a few drops rose water

crystallized rose petals, for decoration

Mix the egg yolks and sugar together in the top of a bain-marie. Bring the milk to the boil. Add the milk to the egg and sugar mixture, a little at a time, stirring constantly over a bain-marie until a custard is formed. Remove the custard from the heat and leave to cool.

•

Put the rose petals in the food processor with a little of the cooled custard and blend. Add the rose petal mixture to the rest of the custard with the rose water. Leave until cold. Freeze in an ice-cream maker.

•

Serve decorated with crystallized rose petals.

•

CRYSTALLIZING ROSE PETALS *The rose petals must be dry. Paint the petals with a little lightly beaten egg white to which a drop or two of rose-water has been added. Gently dip in caster sugar, shake off any excess and leave to dry in a warm place or in the sun.*

CASSATA GELATA

MAKES 1.2 LITRES/2PT

600ml/1pt milk

8 egg yolks

115g/4oz sugar

½ teaspoon pure vanilla essence

30g/1oz roasted almonds, chopped

15g/½oz chopped walnuts

30g/1oz mixed chopped candied peel

15g/½oz chopped candied angelica

30g/1oz natural glacé cherries, chopped

½ teaspoon finely grated lemon peel

¼ wine glass maraschino liqueur

Bring the milk almost to the boil, preferably in a double boiler or bain-marie. Beat the egg yolks with the sugar until fluffy. Whisk in the milk and add the vanilla essence. Return the mixture to the pan and cook stirring until it has thickened enough to coat the back of a wooden spoon. Do not allow the custard to boil or it will curdle. Remove the custard from the heat and cool by standing the pan in a bowl of water topped up with ice. Stir the mixture until it is cooled.

•

Churn in an ice-cream machine for 15–20 minutes. Add the nuts, fruits and liqueur just before the end of churning. Do not add the fruits etc. too early as they will mash too much—the desired effect is to distinguish them in the ice cream.

Honey and Brandy Ice Cream

MAKES 2 LITRES/3½PT

6 eggs, separated

300ml/½pt clear honey

150ml/¼pt brandy

600ml/1pt whipped double cream (preferably Jersey cream)

225g/8oz icing sugar

Beat the egg yolks until they are thick. Beat the egg whites until they are stiff, then fold them together.

•

Mix the remaining ingredients together and fold into the egg mixture. Put in a container and freeze for 4–5 hours before serving. This is a very soft and very rich ice cream.

Fried Ice Cream

GELATO FRITTO

2–3 balls vanilla ice cream per person

crushed amaretti biscuits

icing sugar

ground cinnamon

oil for deep-frying

Batter

self-raising flour

water

Make a light batter and leave to stand for 15 minutes.

•

Roll the ice-cream balls in the amaretti biscuits, dip the balls in the batter and deep-fry in a hot light oil for a few seconds or until the batter is golden and crisp. Drain the balls and dust with icing sugar and cinnamon. Serve immediately. Speed is very important with this recipe. The result is exciting. Do not do too many at a time.

Bilberry Ice Cream

This recipe is basically from Darra Goldstein's book, A Taste of Russia. *In the original recipe blueberries are used.*

●

Crush the berries, with the end of a rolling pin, in a large bowl. Add half the sugar, the vodka and the lemon juice.

●

In the top of a double boiler, put the remaining sugar, salt and egg yolks. Beat until light and fluffy. Gradually add the scalded milk, mixing well. Cook until just thickened, stirring gently with a wooden spoon. Five minutes should be enough; be careful—if overcooked this mixture can curdle. Leave to cool in a bowl of iced water.

●

In a large bowl, beat the soured cream until nearly doubled in volume. Whip the double cream separately until stiff. Carefully fold the soured cream and double cream into the cooled custard mixture. Stir in the bilberries. Churn in an ice-cream maker.

MAKES ABOUT
1.7 LITRES/3PT

450ml/¾pt fresh bilberries

225g/8oz sugar

1 tablespoon vodka

2 teaspoons fresh lemon juice

4 egg yolks

450ml/¾pt milk, scalded

300ml/½pt soured cream

300ml/½pt double cream

pinch of salt

Ricotta Fritters
FRITTELLE DI RICOTTA

SERVES 4–6

225g/8oz ricotta

60g/2oz plain or bitter chocolate, slivered

4 tablespoons caster sugar

2 generous pinches ground cinnamon

4 tablespoons Strega (liqueur)

1 egg

2 eggs, beaten

self-raising flour

light olive oil for deep-frying

icing sugar

Sieve the ricotta into a bowl. Mix the slivered chocolate, sugar, cinnamon, Strega and egg into the ricotta. With 2 spoons, make approximately 20 balls the size of a ping-pong ball. Gently roll the balls in the beaten egg and then in the self-raising flour.

•

Drop the balls into hot olive oil and deep-fry until golden. Dust the ricotta balls with icing sugar and serve at once.

Sweet Fried Zucchini Flowers
FRITTO DI FIORI DI ZUCCHINI DOLCI

This recipe comes from an anonymous cookery book written in 1891 called Il cuoco perfetto marchigiano—*The Perfect Marchigiani Cook.*

•

Make the custard first. Beat the egg yolks, sugar and flour together. Bring the milk to the boil with the lemon peel, lower the heat and slowly add the egg, sugar and flour mixture, stirring continuously. Cook for 10 minutes and keep on stirring. Be careful that the bottom does not catch. Remove from the heat and leave to get cold.

•

Wash and dry the zucchini flowers. Remove the pistules. Fill each flower with 1 tablespoon of the thick confectioner's custard. Gently squeeze the petals together just above the mixture. Dust the flowers first in flour, then dip them in the beaten egg, finishing with the breadcrumbs. A light hand must be used for this exercise.

•

Deep-fry the flowers, in a light olive oil, until golden. Drain on absorbent kitchen paper. Sprinkle the flowers with rum and Alchermes, shake caster sugar over them and serve at once.

SERVES 4

8–12 (male) zucchini flowers, depending on size, but not too open (females have the beginnings of a zucchini, males have only a stem)

Flour

2 eggs, beaten

dry breadcrumbs

light olive oil

rum

Alchermes liqueur

caster sugar

Crema dura (thick confectioner's custard)

5 egg yolks

5 tablespoons sugar

5 tablespoons flour

½ litre/¾pt milk

peel of ½ lemon

DEEP-FRIED FIGS
FRITTURA DI FICHI

SERVES 4

8–12 figs

8–12 teaspoons rum

light olive oil

ground cinnamon

icing sugar

Batter

self-raising flour

water

In years when there is a glut of figs this is a superb way of using them up. These figs are wonderful served with a glass of Moscato d'Ischia or a similar wine.

•

Peel the figs which should be slightly under ripe. Marinate the figs for 1 hour in a teaspoon of rum per fig.

•

Make a light batter and leave it to stand for 15 minutes. Roll the figs in flour then dip them in the light batter. Deep-fry the figs in light olive oil until a pale golden colour. Dust with cinnamon and icing sugar, and serve at once.

STRAWBERRY AND MASCARPONE GRATIN
FRAGOLE E MASCARPONE GRATINATE

SERVES 4

450g/1lb strawberries

225g/8oz mascarpone

2 tablespoons maraschino or kirsch

sugar, white and brown for sprinkling

Slice the strawberries in half into 4 small gratin dishes. Sprinkle white sugar on top to taste, plus the maraschino or kirsch divided evenly between the dishes. Cover with mascarpone and sprinkle with brown sugar. Place under a very hot grill until the sugar is caramelized. Serve hot.

•

This dish can also be made with mixed red fruits.

Grilled Figs with Mascarpone
FICHI CON MASCARPONE

Petal the figs by cutting them in four, not quite through, and pull the skin back from the flesh being very careful not to break it. In the middle of each fig flower put 1 teaspoon of rum, a dusting of cinnamon, then a tablespoon of mascarpone. Sprinkle 1 teaspoon of brown sugar on top of the mascarpone and grill under a very hot grill until the sugar melts. Dust with a little cocoa powder and serve at once.

SERVES 4

8 large ripe figs

1 teaspoon rum per fig

a dusting of freshly ground cinnamon per fig

1 tablespoon mascarpone per fig

1 teaspoon brown sugar per fig

unsweetened cocoa powder

Polenta Fritters
FRITELLE DI POLENTA

If you have any leftover polenta, add enough flour to make a light dough.

•

Roll out the dough in 15cm/6in circles. Do this by breaking off a small chunk and rolling it into a ball, then flattening and rolling it out as thin as a pancake. Fry the polenta pancakes, one at a time, in olive oil, on both sides until crispy. Sprinkle with sugar and eat at once.

THE SNAKE
SERPE

1kg/2$\frac{1}{2}$lb almonds

600g/1lb 4oz sugar

5 egg whites

2 egg yolks

4 teaspoons lemon juice

2 teaspoons vanilla essence

1 tablespoon cinnamon

1 small cup espresso coffee

flour

rice paper

Decoration

2 egg whites

sugar

chocolate hundreds and thousands

silver dragées

1 glacé cherry

1 blanched almond

Blanch the almonds and peel them, toast them in the oven until they are golden all over. Process them in the food processor until they are finely crushed. Transfer the almonds to a bowl and add all the other ingredients, except for the flour and rice paper. Mix thoroughly together.

•

Put a layer of flour $\frac{1}{2}$cm/$\frac{1}{4}$ in thick on a large baking tray and cover with rice paper. Mould the almond mixture into the form of a wriggling snake on the rice paper. Bake in an oven set at 160°C/300°F/gas 2 for an hour, or until it has hardened off. Remove the snake from the oven and leave to cool.

•

To decorate. When cooled, paint the snake with 2 egg whites whipped with a little sugar, sprinkle with some chocolate hundreds and thousands and silver dragées. Use 2 glacé cherry halves for the eyes and a blanched almond for the tongue. Flash in the oven for a minute or two to dry the egg white. Lift gently from the flour and trim off excess rice paper. The snake keeps well for quite a few days.

FILO PASTRY MINCE PIES (WITH VEGETARIAN MINCEMEAT)

This mincemeat improves with maturity and will keep for a long time.

•

Put the cider and sugar in a large saucepan and heat gently until the sugar has dissolved. Add the peeled and diced apples. Stir in the remaining ingredients, except for the rum, and bring slowly to the boil, stirring all the time. Lower the heat under the pan and half cover with a lid. Simmer for 30 minutes until the mixture has become a soft pulp. Remove the mincemeat to a large bowl and leave to get completely cold. Stir in the rum.

•

Spoon into clean, dry screw-top jars, cover with waxed circles before putting on the lids. Store the mincemeat in a cool, dry place.

MINCE PIES

Cut sheets of filo pastry into 9cm/3½in squares. Cover with a dampened cloth. Lightly brush one square of filo pastry with melted unsalted butter which has had the froth removed. Place a second square diagonally on top so that there is a triangle shape on top of a square shape. Lightly brush with melted butter and repeat with another layer but do not butter; the third layer should be placed so that it is a triangle slightly off centre. Try to touch the layers as little as possible, to ensure the pastry is light and crisp.

•

MAKES 3½KG/8LB

450ml/¾pt medium cider

450g/1lb soft dark brown sugar

1.8kg/4lb cooking apples, peeled and diced

1 teaspoon mixed spice

1 teaspoon ground cinnamon

350g/12oz currants

225g/8oz stoned raisins

225g/8oz sultanas

60g/2oz finely chopped candied orange peel

60g/2oz finely chopped candied lemon peel

115g/4oz natural glacé cherries, chopped

finely grated rind and juice of 1 lemon

150ml/¼pt rum

Place the bases in non-stick tart tins, put a little mincemeat in the centre, brush a little butter in a ring on the pastry lid and gently press the buttered part onto the filo base. Brush the top lightly with butter.

•

Bake in an oven set at 190°C/375°F/gas 5 for 8 minutes, until golden brown. Liberally dust the mince pies with icing sugar. These mince pies, which are light and delicate, will have the appearance of Christmas roses.

Carnival Knots

SFRAPPE DI CARNIVALE

500g/1lb 2oz plain white flour

4 eggs whisked with 4 tablespoons of sugar

4 tablespoons virgin olive oil

½ glass milk

½ measure rum

½ measure anisette

a drop or two of vanilla essence

finely grated rind of 1 lemon

Add the eggs and sugar to the flour. Add the virgin olive oil, milk, rum, anisette and vanilla essence. Add the lemon rind. Make a pastry dough and roll out 2–3mm thick. Cut into ribbon strips 2cm/1in wide and 20cm/8in long and tie the ribbons into loose knots. Fry the knots in light olive oil until golden. Drain on kitchen paper and arrange on serving plates. Dust with icing sugar.

•

During our early years at The Walnut Tree we used to celebrate carnivale, *the days leading up to Lent. All our staff wore Italian regional costumes and we cooked regional Italian dishes. The dining room, bistro and bar were festooned with brightly coloured paper garlands and one of the local Italian farmers played his accordian.*

Fig Salami

FRUSTRINGO (LONZA DI FICHI)

Mince the figs, add all the other ingredients and mix thoroughly. Divide the mixture into 5 parts. Dust a board and your hands with icing sugar and roll out salamis 5cm/2in wide and 28cm/11in long. Wrap in rice paper and then parcel up in greaseproof paper. Leave to mature in a dry cool place for about 1 month before using. After 1 month, wrap the salamis in foil. Store in a dry place.

•

A slice or two of lonza di fichi *is good served with pecorino cheese. Originally it was eaten with a slice of bread as a snack.*

2kg/4½lb dried honey figs, no flour dusted on top

200g/7oz almonds, roughly chopped

200g/7oz walnuts, roughly chopped

150g/5oz natural candied peel, finely chopped

400g/14oz chopped dates

100g/3½oz whole pistachios

200g/7oz bitter chocolate, chopped

1 liqueur glass brandy

1 liqueur glass Strega

1 liqueur glass anisette

1 liqueur glass crème de menthe

2 teaspoons freshly ground cinnamon

1 tablespoon vanilla essence

CANARINO

SMALL CANARY—A LEMON DRINK

Before squeezing the juice from the lemons wash them thoroughly. Then with a sharp knife, pare the skin from the fruit to make a long spiral. Endeavour to peel the lemon peel in one go. Try not to cut into the pith. Place lemon spirals in a Russian glass teacup, pour boiling water over and leave to infuse for 4–5 minutes. This makes a very soothing drink, either hot or cold.

•

Unwaxed lemons are advisable for this drink.

WALNUT LIQUEUR

NOCINO

25 green walnuts, quartered

200g/7oz sugar

1 litre/1¾pt grappa

½ lemon

50g/1½oz cinnamon

½ vanilla pod

pinch of fennel seed

1 piece mace

Tradition has it that this liqueur must be made on the 24 June, the feast of St John. Put the walnuts in a large glass jar and add all the other ingredients. Cover the jar with a strong piece of paper, tie it on and make a small hole with a pin. Wrap the jar in thick black paper, and leave in the sun for 40 days. The black paper is to absorb as much warmth as possible on cooler days. After 40 days, filter the liqueur and put it in bottles. Seal them well.

INDEX